To _____

From _____

My Favorite Recipe:

Signed _____

Date _____

FAMOUS
florida!™

UNDERGROUND GOURMET
RESTAURANTS, RECIPES & REFLECTIONS

Text by Barbie Baldwin

Cover Art and Illustrations by Pat Stockey

™ LaFray Publishing Company

First Edition
FOR ADDITIONAL COPIES, USE ORDER BLANKS IN
THE BACK OF THE BOOK OR WRITE DIRECTLY TO:

LaFray Publishing Company
P.O. Box 7326
St. Petersburg, Florida 33734

Printed in the United States of America

International Standard Book Number: 0-942-084-01-2
Library of Congress Card Catalog Number: 82-082923

First Printing: September 1982
0 9 8 7 6 5 4 3

Publisher: *Joyce LaFray*
Text By: *Barbie Baldwin*
Edited By: *bj Altschul*
Joyce LaFray
Food Consultant: *Holly Audsley*
Typography: *Media Graphics*

FAMOUS FLORIDA!™ **Underground Gourmet** *introduces you to the best of Florida's down-home, backwoods restaurants.*

If you can take your own driving tour, as we have, please do. Dress casually — a T-shirt and jeans will be just fine. Or take your tour through **FAMOUS FLORIDA!**™ *We've included the most outstanding recipes given us by the owners of these great eating houses themselves.*

The restaurants, which we've carefully selected, are more than just eating establishments. They're statements of Florida's heritage, with fascinating stories about the state's past, its traditions in food preparation, customs and folks who have relocated here.

One of the trademarks of each restaurant included is the personal interest the owners take in all of their customers, and this feature should be part of your preparation, too, whenever you fix any of the **Underground Gourmet** *courses.*

Whether you enjoy these recipes at the restaurants or at home, we know you'll enjoy your tour of **FAMOUS FLORIDA!**™

Joyce LaFray
Publisher

Notes From The Test Kitchen

FAMOUS FLORIDA!™ Underground Gourmet *offers you a most distinctive eating and cooking experience.*

We'd like to suggest that you not judge how a recipe is going to taste by its list of ingredients, as many of these may be different from your usual bill of fare. Be adventurous! Try them so you can get a real taste of our state's native cuisine.

Whenever special or unusual ingredients are listed, we have suggested substitutions that you can readily find. However, some of the unusual ingredients — cooter, armadillo and rattlesnake, for instance — are not available at your local market, so your best bet may be to experience these culinary delights at the restaurants themselves.

If you **do** *plan on hunting some of the native fare yourself, be sure to check with county government regarding local regulations. For instance, the Sabal Palm (as used in our Swamp Cabbage recipe) is not a* **state** *protected species, but many* **counties** *in Florida regulate and protect the species. Substitutions are suggested for your convenience.*

All of the fine recipes we've included have been carefully selected and tested and, in many cases, reduced from very large quantities to suit your needs. If you already have a basic knowledge of cooking you'll find them easy to prepare. Serving suggestions and other helpful hints are also provided. Our comments, after testing, are in italics at the bottom of each recipe. We had a great time testing these recipes. Since this will be a new experience for many of you, be prepared for some fantastic results and great eating!

Holly Audsley
Food Consultant

(Holly Audsley holds a Bachelor's Degree in Home Economics and is a well-known lecturer and food demonstrator in the Tampa Bay area.)

DEDICATION

To Rick, my husband, and all the other Florida "Crackers," whose insatiable appetite and appreciation of traditional eatin' off the beaten path proves that "The Other Florida" still exists.

Introduction

Cruising the Interstate from attraction to attraction, you might easily miss a part of Florida obscured by growth and modern construction. That heritage and the native traditions that are passed on through oral histories and home-style meals are the heart of **FAMOUS FLORIDA!**™ **Underground Gourmet**.

The initial criteria for restaurants to be included was low-cost, home-cooked meals in places with lots of character. As our search expanded, though, so did the list of criteria, soon to include restaurants that serve original Floridian foods and whose owners grew up in the state, with stories to tell of its past.

The result is a compilation of native recipes, recipes developed from the many ethnic influences in the state, stories of Florida's early development, short profiles of some of the people who helped settle the rugged regions, and suggestions for enjoying the communities near the restaurants themselves.

For every restaurant selected, a dozen could well have been chosen, if time and space had been available. Our choices are based on recommendations from food editors around the state, travelers, salespeople, business executives, media reps, city employees, friends — all people you might encounter on a typical day anywhere in the state — and a few "accidental" discoveries.

Most of the restaurants included feature inexpensive meals, and some are downright low-priced. The few that are average in price are exceptional for the quantity or quality of food served. Where menu items are described, you'll become familiar with the type of food served by that particular restaurant, but if the dish you read about is not on the menu when you visit, don't worry — it may have been replaced with one you'll enjoy even more.

As you take your tour of Florida through the restaurants included in this book, you'll also experience the influences of geography and climate on our food. Florida could well be called the melting pot of the nation, its kettle filled with Spanish, Greek, Minorcan, French, Caribbean, Cuban, Creole, Deep South and "Cracker" traditions. Add to this a climate which produces a greater variety and abundance of fruits and vegetables year 'round than anywhere else in the world plus the great variety of fish inhabiting our waters — and there you have it, a most irresistible place to live!

Many of the restaurants and their owners featured in **FAMOUS FLORIDA!**™ **Underground Gourmet** are preserving a slice of Americana that may well be considered an endangered species. Take time now to visit them **now**, for, like the words in Joni Mitchell's song,

> "Don't it always seem to go,
> that you don't know what you've got 'til it's gone."

When you create these recipes for your family or guests, do share with them the stories of their origin and creators. Together we can keep Florida's heritage and traditions alive.

Table of Contents

FAMOUS
florida! T.M.

Our sincere thanks to all of the restaurant owners and managers featured in this book for sharing their favorite recipes with us, without whom this book would not have been possible.

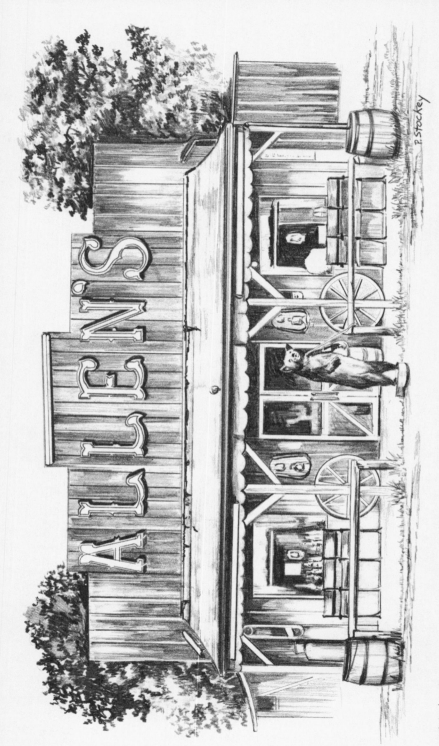

ALLEN'S

P. Stockey

Allen's Historical Cafe, Auburndale, Florida

Allen's Historical Cafe

— Auburndale —

Carl Allen, owner of Allen's Historical Cafe, is a prime example of what this book is all about. One of the first to be interviewed, he serves as an inspiration throughout *FAMOUS FLORIDA!* "Underground Gourmet." Hearing his stories filled me with laughter and tears, literally. And when I left, I felt I was saying goodbye to a dear friend.

Carl Allen was born in Auburndale, just 15 miles east of Lakeland. Like any other little boy, one of his favorite preoccupations was excavating in the dirt. When he was just 10, he uncovered three pieces of metal, somewhat like tools, but like nothing he had ever seen before. His excitement and curiosity over the purpose of his find became a lifelong ambition. He's been chasing and uncovering the past ever since.

His restaurant bears testimony to his conviction to discover, preserve and share our ancestry. There are literally thousands of artifacts on display, decorating the walls, even serving useful purposes in the restaurant. The tables are made from antique sewing machines...you can even pump the pedals while you eat. The entire restaurant is a living legend, an educational experience that far surpasses a place to get something good to eat. Carl has made it easy on the "microwave generation" by adding notecards of explanation for many of the artifacts. And the lounge area, the breeding ground for up-and-coming bluegrass bands, is furnished with tables that feature different historical themes such as Gunfighters, Confederates, Cowboys, Indians, Old Trains, and Gone With the Wind. Carl made them himself with authentic artifacts covered by epoxy resin.

The menu is as filled with Florida's past as the atmosphere of this museum/eatery. Rattlesnake, soft shell turtle (cooter), swamp cabbage, Nile perch and grits are a few of the dishes to sample. Rattlesnake is a sweet white meat, with texture and flavor similar to frog legs. To Carl's knowledge, his is the only establishment serving it in Florida. He has local hunters bring the rattlesnakes to him alive, so that he is sure the meat is fresh. He might even go into the kitchen during your visit to "take care of" a six-footer.

Soft shell turtle, usually called cooter, is the texture of chicken, but with a flavor all its own. Carl says it is not anything like the sea turtle commonly served in resort restaurants.

The Green's Salad, made from Florida's abundant avocado, mixed with pecans and purple grapes, is one of those rich, delicious dishes that you can nutritionally justify. It's made from an old, old recipe that true Florida "crackers" were raised on.

Though everything on the menu is exceptional, the swamp cabbage is what gastronomic dreams are made of. Relatively few Florida residents or guests have had the pleasure, as the cabbage palm is grown only in Florida and is, in fact, the state tree. The rich and flavorful vegetable, made from the tender heart of this type of palm, was first prepared by Indians long before the Spaniards arrived. Swamp cabbage doesn't taste like any other vegetable you've tried but may soon top your list of favorites.

Carl Allen's Cafe and cooking are totally Florida — not shell shops or "freebie" orange juice stands. You won't find anything on the menu that wasn't grown, caught, netted, raised, or hatched in this state. Oh, that doesn't mean there aren't some less exotic dishes for the less adventurous. You'll find Southern Fried Chicken and meat-and-potato type dinners. That's real Florida, too.

But, back to Carl Allen. He *is* the restaurant, even more

than his food. A living testimony to the Florida that was and, if one oasis of Florida's past is proof of its existence, still is. To most of today's Auburndale residents, Carl is considered to be a town forefather. It was in this quaint community named by the first settlers for Auburndale, Massachusetts, that he found his first artifacts that are now displayed in the restaurant.

Carl was recently selected Florida's "#1 Cracker" by the state Sertoma Club, of which he is an active member. As he explains it, the term originally was used to describe Florida cowboys who would crack their whips while rustling scrub cows. These 300-pound cows were the cowboys' and Indians' protein. The term was also used to describe Georgia migrant workers, "corn crackers" who were considered to be shiftless people. That's the origin of the song, "...Jimmy crack corn and I don't care..." A true "Florida Cracker" like Carl Allen, who *was* at one time a Florida cowboy rustling scrub cows, is careful to make a distinction between the two. The word is now used to describe the precious few who were born and raised here.

Proud of his Florida heritage, Carl feels Florida's settlers were the strongest of this country's founders and that it is unfortunate that history books concentrate on the development of the Old West during that era, with little attention being given to the deep South of the mid-1800s. Central Florida's ancestors were driven here by the aftermath of the Civil War to begin new lives. Many of these settlers were widows, including Carl's own grandmother, angry over the destruction of their homes and the death of their men. But he credits this anger with the determination that was necessary to conquer a rugged, unsettled region that was wilderness up until 40 years ago. He also credits these women with keeping Florida's food traditions alive as there was little else for them to do in this socially inactive region but to exchange recipes and discover natural vegetation safe for consumption. The strength of character of today's Central Florida "crackers" — stern, honest and kind — can be attributed to their grandmothers, he says.

Carl is as obsessed with chasing the past as he is with sharing it and preserving it. Once each year he invites senior citizens to "eat with him" without charge so that they can all share stories of Florida's past, to keep our heritage alive.

He also shares Florida's history in lectures to area schools and state organizations and says that in his travels he is finding younger generations now very interested in preserving Florida's ecological balance.

Yet despite this wide variety of interests and activities (he also writes poetry and newspaper columns), Carl Allen still manages to make his 22-year-old restaurant in Auburndale his first priority.

"If people come all the way over here to eat with me, I want to be here to sit with them," he says. If everyone were like Carl and took the time to pass his mind on to another, no one would need to search for the meaning of life. He has found meaning and has it to share, giving us a tangible feeling of pride in the heritage of this state.

How to get there: 1387 U.S. Hwy. 92 West, Auburndale. Take Interstate 4 to Lakeland. Exit on U.S. 98 southbound to U.S. 92. Go east approximately 12 miles until you see a bear standing on the front porch of a little wood house with "Allen's" on the roof.

While you're here: If you make it on a weekend you'll be entertained with some of the finest bluegrass music you will ever hear. Jamming at "Catfish Carl's" is a popular activity with locals. Carl also coordinates several special bluegrass concerts, including the Florida Bluegrass Championships held in March. You might give him a call to find out exactly when they are scheduled. And, if you've ever wondered where you could go to get in on a real old-fashioned Fourth of July celebration, Auburndale is the place. The entire area turns out for a full weekend of festivities. Ever seen a Walking Catfish Race? They do it here. The fish actually walk to the finish line! You're right . . . you will have to see it to believe it. So do!

GREEN'S SALAD
(Florida Avocado & Grape Salad)

1	lb. large, purple grapes (peeled and seeds removed)
1	medium sized avocado (peeled and cut in 1¼" chunks)
½	c. pecans (chopped fine)
1	T. mayonnaise
3-4	T. sour cream
	small dash sweetener

1. Combine grapes and avocado in small bowl.
2. Mix remaining ingredients together and pour over fruit. Toss lightly to coat all.
3. Serve immediately.

Serves: 6
Preparation: 20 minutes

"A delightfully refreshing salad — perfect for Florida living!"

— NOTES —

ALLEN'S HISTORICAL CAFE
AUBURNDALE

HUSHPUPPIES
(Allow to Chill Overnight)

2   T. sugar
¼   c. onions (minced)
2   c. yellow corn meal
1   c. white corn meal
½   T. salt
½   T. black pepper
1   t. baking powder
1½   c. buttermilk
      fat for frying

1. Mix all ingredients, except buttermilk and fat in large bowl.
2. Add buttermilk just until mixture is of a consistency to be rolled into small balls.
3. Let stand in refrigerator overnight. Can be kept in refrigerator, covered for several days.
4. Roll into small balls and drop into fat heated to 250°F. Cook until brown.

Makes: 4-5 dozen
Preparation: Chill overnight/10 minutes
Cooking: 15 minutes

"Fry up a batch and serve them with your favorite dish!"

— NOTES —

ALLEN'S CATFISH

small channel catfish, cleaned and scaled
salt
pepper
Accent
meal mixture
cooking oil for frying (Wesson or peanut oil)

— MEAL MIXTURE —
1	**lb. yellow corn meal**
½	**lb. white corn meal**
1	**t. salt**
½	**t. black pepper**

— MEAL MIXTURE —
1. Mix all meal mixture ingredients together. (They can be stored in airtight container in refrigerator for several weeks.)
   — FISH —
2. Sprinkle salt, pepper, and Accent over fish. Coat in meal mixture.
3. Drop in oil heated to 350°F. Cook until nice and brown. (About 10-12 minutes.)

Serves: 1-2 fish per person
Preparation: 10 minutes
Cooking: 15 minutes

"One of Florida's favorite foods ... And will soon be one of yours also!"

— NOTES —

RATTLESNAKE
(Allow to Freeze Overnight)

1   **rattlesnake**
1   **egg (beaten)**
     breading mix
     oil or Crisco for frying

1. Take the rattlesnake and lay it on a cutting board.
2. Remove the head plus at least two inches into the body in order to remove all poisons. Then run a knife along the belly of the snake (the skin comes off quite easily).
3. Clean out the inside of the snake and cut it into about 3″ pieces. Freeze these overnight.
4. When ready to prepare, remove from freezer. Allow to thaw slightly. Dip in egg, and breading mix.
5. Deep fat fry for 20 minutes in fat heated to 300°F.
6. The meat is similar to chicken or frog legs but very boney. Eat by picking the meat off the bones.

NOTE: Unless you are an expert rattlesnake hunter, we advise you NOT to hunt your own. A trip to Allen's may be your best bet on this one.

Serves: 4 oz. lean meat per serving
Preparation: Freeze overnight/20 minutes
Cooking: 20 minutes

"No wonder Rattlesnake hunts are so popular!"

— NOTES —

ARMADILLO

1	armadillo
2	c. water
¼	c. vinegar
	salt
	pepper
	flour
1-2	eggs (beaten)
	cooking oil for frying

1. To clean armadillo, hull from shell and remove tough skin from underside.
2. Combine water and vinegar in large bowl. Place meat in liquids to marinate for a few minutes.
3. Cut meat into small pieces, about 2″ across.
4. Salt and pepper meat. Dip into flour, then into beaten egg, and back into flour.
5. Deep fat fry in cooking oil heated to 300°F for 20-25 minutes or until tender when tested with fork.

Serves: 4 oz. meat per serving
Preparation: 15 minutes
Cooking: 25 minutes

"Armadillo meat is somewhat dark in color but has a good flavor, resembling that of turtle! Come on, try it."

— NOTES —

COOTER (SOFT SHELL TURTLE)

3-4 turtles* (2 lbs.)
    salt and pepper
    Accent
    flour
1   egg (beaten)
½   c. milk
    fat for frying (enough to cover the turtles)

1. Take the turtles, turn them upside down and peel out the meat (like you peel an orange).
2. Clean it and cut it into small pieces.
3. Sprinkle with salt, pepper, and Accent.
4. Dip in flour, then in mixture of egg and milk, then back in flour.
5. Deep fat fry in fat heated to 300°F until done or southern fry in gravy.

Serves: 6
Preparation: 25 minutes
Cooking: 15-20 minutes

*Cooter is tender, unlike the sea turtle found in many Florida lakes.

"Has a similar taste to chicken but a lot better!"

— NOTES —

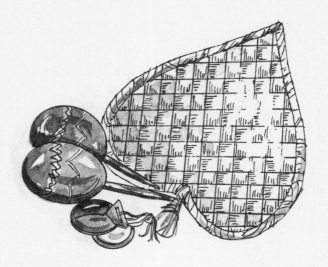

The Lincoln Restaurant

— Tampa —

There is no greater ethnic influence on Florida's food traditions than that contributed by the state's large population of Latin Americans. Since 1513, when the Spanish explorer Ponce de Leon discovered *La Florida*, meaning the flowered state, Spanish traditions have influenced all walks of Florida life.

One of the areas where Latin American food preparation is most alive and appreciated, is in Tampa. Since Tampa's Spanish settlers developed a brisk trade with Cuba in the 1800s, the combination of the two regions has benefited the Bay Area with a delicious blend of distinctive cuisine.

Though Ybor City, a Spanish community in the heart of Tampa, is nationally famous for its restaurants and shops, there is another "underground gourmet" community of excellent Latin American restaurants just west of Ybor City, referred to as "Boliche Boulevard." It is here, where Columbus Drive meets

Lincoln Avenue, that you will discover one of the best and least expensive of the dozens of these gourmet ethnic eateries in the Tampa Bay area.

The Lincoln Restaurant, named for its location rather than composition, offers a complete menu of both Spanish and Cuban dishes.

Its owners, Lali and Glenn Fulgueira, combine a dedication to authenticity of their cuisine with a warm hospitality and patience with guests who can decipher only the ingredients of Yellow Rice and Chicken on the menu.

Lali and Glenn, and parents on both sides, were born and raised in Tampa. Both sets of grandparents, however, were born in Spain. Lali's parents opened the restaurant in 1963. In 1974 Lali and Glenn took over the ownership, though her mother still lends a hand when needed.

The lunch menu is different each day of the week but always features three soups, a special, and 13 entree choices. The dinner menu offers nearly 40 entrees, served with two vegetables, a salad and Cuban bread.

One of the house specialties is Paella. The Spanish feast combines lobster, shrimp, fish fillet, clams, stone crabs, scallops, chicken and fresh pork baked with yellow rice, onions, peppers and pimiento. It is made only for two or more people and requires 45 minutes to prepare but is well worth the wait.

A popular appetizer is Caldo Gallego, a soup of collard greens, beans, potatoes and Chorizo, a Spanish sausage. You can also choose Spanish Bean (Garbanzo) Soup or Shrimp Al Ajillo.

Other entrees include Stuffed Trout, baked in wine with a papillote stuffing; Filete Salteado, beef tenderloin cubed and sauteed in wine, olive oil, chopped onions, green pepper, Chorizo and Ham, served with yellow rice; Carne Con Papas (Spanish Beef Stew); Mondongo Andaluza (honeycomb beef tripe); Ropa Veija, shredded beef in a spicy tomato sauce; and Boliche. Boliche is the dish that named this Boulevard. It is an eye of round stuffed with bacon, ham or Chorizo. Here, they use bacon or salt pork, as Lali claims the ham and Chorizo overpower the flavor of the meat.

Most of the entrees come with two vegetables from a dozen alternatives including yellow rice, Spanish fries, black beans, platanos, and Yuca con Mojo, which is the yuca plant root sauteed in olive oil, lemon and garlic.

Top off your meal with Flan, Guava Shells and Cream Cheese, Cheesecake or Spanish Cream. The closest thing to compare the Spanish Cream to is the rich cream between the pastry layers of a French Napoleon, which the Spanish call a Senorita. Its appearance, with a burned sugar topping, may remind you of a burnt-edge lemon cookie, pudding style.

If you don't need eight hours of sleep, accompany your dessert with a cup of Cuban coffee. The potent concoction requires at least a half cup of milk to get it down, according to Lali.

The Lincoln Restaurant also offers a children's menu, though the entire menu is "half-pint" priced.

The decor of the 100-seat restaurant is quite contemporary with paneled walls, grass fans and dried flowers, matching tablecloths, comfortable seating and English-speaking waitresses without an accent. Regardless of your ethnic background, you will feel very comfortable here, even if you ask your waitress for a "blow-by-blow" description of everything on the menu. You won't have to order black beans and yellow rice just because it sounds safe. If the decor lacks ethnic authenticity, it is compensated by the food, which is very uncompromising, plentiful, delicious, and incredibly inexpensive. Everyone is served *con gusto*, with pleasure.

Each year in February, Tampa surrenders to "pirates" who re-invade the city in a full-rigged pirate ship. Though this re-enactment of the invasion of the 19th century Spanish buccaneer, Jose Gaspar, occurs just one day a year during the city's Gasparilla Festival, Tampa residents and guests willingly surrender every day of the year to the city's many excellent Spanish restaurants, for which The Lincoln is an excellent representative.

How to get there: 3247 W. Columbus Drive, Tampa. Take Interstate 275 to the Dale Mabry exit. Turn north to Columbus and east three blocks. The restaurant is near the Tampa Stadium, but not open on Sundays.

While you're here: Once you have familiarized yourself with Spanish/ Cuban cuisine at the Lincoln Restaurant, you can do your own gourmet discovery tour in Ybor City, just ten minutes east of here. Ybor City, once the cigar capital of the world and still known for cigar production, gave Tampa its CB handle of "Cigar City." The small Latin American community is filled with shops and restaurants.

YELLOW RICE

¼	c. olive oil
1	Spanish onion (diced)
1	green pepper (diced)
1	clove garlic (crushed)
2	bay leaves
1	pinch oregano
2	t. salt
½	t. pepper
1	tomato (diced — may substitute 2 canned whole tomatoes crushed)
2	c. water (can include juice from canned tomatoes)
1	c. long grain rice (do not use converted)
2	drops yellow food coloring
	peas and pimiento (garnish)

1. Heat oil in large skillet. Add next 8 ingredients. Saute until tender.
2. Add water. Bring to boil. Add rice and food coloring.
3. Bring to boil again. Stir. Cover and bake in oven at 375°F for 20 minutes. Or cook on top of stove at medium-low for 20 minutes.
4. Garnish with peas and pimiento. Serve.

Serves: 4 as side dish; 2 as entree with meat
Preparation: 5 minutes
Cooking: 30 minutes

"Perfect with chicken!"

— NOTES —

CARNE CON PAPAS (SPANISH BEEF STEW)

1   lb. top round cubes
      olive oil for sauteing
2   t. salt
1   t. pepper
1   clove garlic (crushed)
1   28 oz. can whole tomatoes (crushed with hand)
1   large Spanish onion (chopped)
1   large green pepper (chopped)
2   T. oregano
3   bay leaves
3   medium potatoes (cubed)
3   T. flour
¼   c. water
Optional: 4 carrots (sliced)
         1 — 1 lb. can string beans

1. Place olive oil in large, deep skillet or dutch oven along with meat, salt, pepper, garlic. Brown well.
2. Add tomatoes, onion and green pepper. Cook for few minutes longer.
3. Add oregano and bay leaves. Bring to boil.
4. Reduce heat to slow simmer. Cook for 30 minutes.
5. Add potatoes and cook until meat and potatoes are tender (about 30 minutes).
6. Mix flour and water together. Add to stew. Stir until thickened.
   *NOTE: If adding optional ingredients, add carrots with potatoes and add beans near end of cooking to heat through.

Serves: 4
Preparation: 15 minutes
Cooking: 1 hour 15 minutes

"Delicious served with hard rolls. Sop up the delectable juice. Serve with tossed green salad!"

SPANISH CREAM

1	qt. milk
⅛	t. salt
1	cinnamon stick
	rind of ¼-½ lemon (keep whole but do not get into the bitter white layer)
3	eggs
½	c. cornstarch
1	c. sugar
1	T. vanilla
2	drops yellow food coloring
	sugar for topping

1. Bring milk to a boil with salt, cinnamon, and lemon rind in large saucepan.
2. In another saucepan combine all other ingredients, except sugar for topping, and mix very, very well.
3. Take cinnamon stick and lemon rind out of milk.
4. Put egg mixture over low heat and let it heat up slightly. While stirring, slowly pour milk into eggs and continue to cook until thick and bubbly.
5. Pour into 9x11" cake pan. Sprinkle sugar over top and allow it to sink in. Chill.

Serves: 6-8
Preparation: 10 minutes
Cooking: 30 minutes

"This dish is especially attractive if the top is burned with a special instrument found in gourmet shops!"

— NOTES —

Mel's Hot Dogs

"The dog is the noblest of all animals, and the hot dog is the noblest of all dogs, because it, and it alone, feeds the hand that bites it."
— Mel Lohn

— Tampa —

Nobody knows, understands, and loves dogs like Mel Lohn, owner and chef extraordinaire of Mel's Hot Dogs in Tampa.

In one hour, he'll tell you more about hot dogs than you ever imagined there was to know, or cared to know, about them. Mel explains that 99% of the hot dogs on today's market are the skinless type, composed of either meat plus fillers such as chicken, pork, or beef plus soybean or artificial "extenders"; or they are all-meat, but not necessarily beef. Not only does this type of hot dog have little flavor to begin with, but what flavor and natural juices do exist, get lost in the cooking process because there is nothing to keep them in.

"One all-beef hot dog, special mustard sauce, onions, sauerkraut, relish and pickle on a poppy seed bun."

Mel's hot dogs, in contrast, are kosher-style whole beef cuts, hand-stuffed into natural casings and slowly smoked. Mel says the natural casing gives you the "pop" when you take the first bite, followed by an explosion of juices with incredible flavor.

The hot dogs, special "square" poppy seed buns, and kosher relish all arrive directly from Chicago, Mel's former habitat. Beef from the Midwest, where cattle are corn-fed, makes all the difference in the world, he says.

"Love me, love my dog."

Mel is a story all in himself. He is at least half the reason for the restaurant's success. The other half is his dogs. Mel is animated and witty and walks a thin line between unique and bizarre. His zany personality would appear more appropriate in a position such as a talk show host, radio announcer or circus barker. What's a crazy guy like Mel doing in a place like this?

He arrived in this area ten years ago, touring with a rock band as their sax player, spending most of his free time searching for a hot dog like those back home. Alas, a search in vain. But he did love the weather. So, when his band returned to the Midwest, Mel stayed behind. In order to accommodate his hot dog habit and fill a void in the "wiener-weak" area, he opened up Mel's Red Hot Ranch. "Red Hots" is "Chicago-ese" for hot dogs.

He readily admits a long-term love affair with the hot dog. After all, he says, you are what you eat. Thousands of Mel's baskets are served each day. The menu features Mel's Special Hot Dog Basket, with fabulous crispy fries, and six variations including his Chili Dog, Slaw Dog and the Mighty Mel. Other menu options include Italian Steak and Sausage baskets and hamburger baskets. Chili, cole slaw and onion rings are side order selections. Beer and wine are also available.

A stickler for quality in his food, its appearance, and the level of personal service, Mel says attitude is his first priority when he hires his staff. He believes that making people feel at home is what brings them back. When you place your order, you give your first name. When your order is up, your name is called out, no numbers. That way, Mel and his true-blue manager of nine years get to know you as well as you know them.

He's so much of a people-pleaser that his Red Hot Ranch is now called simply Mel's Hot Dogs. "That is what everyone was calling it, so I just changed the name to suit them," he says.

The decor is mostly Mel. The walls are covered with dozens

of framed articles of acclaim from local and national publications. An ABC news representative, who had just completed a lengthy tour of Europe, wrote that, in all confidence, he could declare Mel's hot dog *the* top dog in the world, including Frankfurt, Germany, where he had expected to find the best. In addition to the articles, many local artists have chosen Mel as the perfect subject for caricatures. Their work provides an entertaining visual while your taste buds are enjoying themselves.

Had Lord Byron been a part of this era, it would have been Mel's that inspired him to write that a dog "in life is the firmest friend."

How to get there: 4136 E. Busch Blvd., Tampa. From I-75 north or southbound, take the Busch Boulevard exit, east. Mel's is on the north side of the boulevard, approximately one mile east of Busch Gardens.

While you're here: Visit Busch Gardens, 40th Street and Busch Boulevard. The Dark Continent is the second most popular tourist attraction in the state. The 300-acre resort brings the Africa of yesteryear alive through desert traders, open-air bazaar, wild animals roaming the Serengeti Plain and an amusement park that delivers the mystery and excitement of the jungle. Busch's Adventure Island, a fabulous water-fun park is just a few blocks from the gardens.

MEL'S SPRITE® SANGRIA
(Allow Time To Soak Overnight)

3   liters red burgundy wine (use a good one!)
4   oz. orange juice (fresh, but may substitute frozen)
3   oz. lemon juice (fresh, but may substitute frozen)
¾   c. sugar
2   t. cinnamon (ground)
1   liter Sprite®

1. Mix all ingredients except Sprite® to form a concentrated mixture. Soak overnight.
2. To serve, mix ⅓ Sprite® to ⅔ of the concentrated mixture for each serving.
3. Garnish with sliced fruit.
4. Pour into large pitcher fill with ice and serve.

Serves: 12-8 oz. servings.
Preparation: When made ahead, 2 minutes.

You'll want to make this Sprite® away."

— NOTES —

MEL'S SPECIAL HOT DOG BASKET

1   natural casing kosher hot dog
1   poppy seed hot dog bun (from bakery)
2   T. kosher sauerkraut
2   T. kosher relish
2   T. Bermuda onion (chopped)
1   t. mustard
1   kosher pickle, sliced lengthwise

1.   Steam hot dog in covered container using a vegetable steamer or similar device.
2.   Heat bun until steamy. Place hot dog in bun. Arrange garnishes on top.
3.   Serve in basket with crispy french fries made from premium quality Idaho Potatoes, fried in all-vegetable shortening.

Serves: 1
Preparation: 10 minutes
Cooking time: 5 minutes

"Hot Dog!"

— NOTES —

MEL'S MOTHER'S COLE SLAW

1½   lb. purple cabbage
1   medium carrot (½ c. shredded)
1   c. mayonnaise
¼   c. white vinegar
1   T. sugar
1   t. celery seed
      seasoned salt to taste

1.   Shred cabbage and carrot in shredder or food processor.
2.   Mix juices and seasonings. Pour over cabbage and carrot. Mix well. Refrigerate for half-hour before serving.

Serves: 6-8
Preparation: 20 minutes
Chill: 30 minutes

"Vinegar gives the salad a nice tangy flavor!"

— NOTES —

The Rib Junction

— Land O' Lakes —

Up to their elbows in barbecue sauce is how Ralph and Nancy Shumaker like to see their customers at The Rib Junction. It's the kind of place where you don't have to worry too much about manners — just roll up your sleeves, dig in and enjoy some of the tastiest ribs around.

As partner Mike Hogan says, they want to be — and are — known for big portions, and a limited menu "that's the best in town. We want everyone to walk out with a smile on their face," he says.

And indeed they do. Even the very first day The Rib Junction opened, so the story goes, customers enjoyed the ribs and chicken so much that the restaurant had to close earlier in the evening than their posted hours because they ran out of food.

Now, you might wonder, what is there in Land O' Lakes that would make so many folks so hungry for good ribs? Actually, Ralph, Nancy and Mike invented a new town name, "Land O' Lutz," because they're located right at the junction of Land O' Lakes and Lutz. They figured that, with a Land O' Lakes address and a Lutz phone number, they'd have insulted residents of one town or the other if they had spread the word that they were in one town and didn't mention the other. So they coined a new name instead.

And located about a 15-minute ride north of Tampa, The Rib Junction is far enough out of the urban area that it's almost the only game in the countryside. When word got around there was going to be a *real* rib place, the public was ready. Mike says their advertising is primarily word of mouth and the "smoke drifting out over Hwy. 41." With something like a million cars a month crossing the "apex" intersection of 41 and Dale Mabry, plenty of people found out about RJ pretty quickly.

The Junction came into being when Mike and Ralph, both builders, were working on a construction project together. When they finished the job they "got to talkin' about this place" and in 24 hours had bought it. They decided to give it a try even though they had little previous restaurant experience — Ralph had come from South Carolina and was an excellent finish carpenter, and Mike's family had moved from Ohio to relocate their dairy farm business.

They refinished the building, modified the existing open pit to suit their needs, and experimented with sauces, meats, and serving sizes for a month before finally opening their doors. The effort paid off.

"Controlling the fire is the most important part of cooking ribs," Mike says. "If we cook 'em too fast they get burnt and tough. If we cook 'em too slow, we can't keep up with serving. So we rotate their elevation from the fire, something we learned only by practice."

The pit itself is special. It's constructed of silver Zerian stone, made by a specialist whose trademark is to mark one stone in every pit he makes with an arrowhead shape and an etching of a primitive man spearing a wild hog. The mantelpiece is red western cedar, and the interior of the pit is "three-sided" native Florida cypress — plain on two sides, cut on one, with the bark left on only one side. What's nice about cypress, Mike points out, is that it doesn't rot and doesn't attract termites.

As for cooking the ribs, he adds, the quality of the fire comes from using native Florida woods, blackjack oak, dry orange, and a little green hickory mixed in slowly.

Besides the extra-meaty ribs, the pork roast sandwich is the RJ's best seller, with a monstrous serving of pork on giant buns baked fresh at a Cuban bakery. Whether you go for the ribs, chicken, or pork sandwich, you can have it served with the sauce on top, on the side, or, if you prefer, with hot sauce. Baked beans and cole slaw come with every meal; the secret to the beans is that they're cooked in cast-iron pots, on the fire, for a long time. Top it all off with Nancy's own homemade cheesecake, so popular that sometimes Ralph has to take a day off just to help her finish making all the special orders.

It's no surprise The Rib Junction caught on the way it did. When Ralph and Mike first opened, they took advantage of the season, anticipating a slowdown when the "snowbirds" went back home. But the slowdown never came, because the regulars, many of whom preferred to go there when it was quieter (or so they thought), started bringing all *their* friends along.

It's been non-stop ever since.

How to get there: From Tampa, drive north on U.S. 41 or Dale Mabry Highway, just past the County Line Road that separates Hillsborough and Pasco counties. The Rib Junction is on the right; if you get to S.R. 54, you've gone too far.

While you're here: This is an as yet relatively undeveloped area that's pleasant to drive around just to look at the farmland on a relaxing afternoon. If it's excitement you're after, drive back into Tampa and visit Busch Gardens, one of the state's most popular attractions.

PICNIC BAKED BEANS

55 oz. can Bush's Best canned beans
1 small Spanish onion (diced)
¼ c. dark brown sugar
1-2 T. Gulden's brown mustard
2 T. molasses
1-2 T. soy sauce
2 T. Worcestershire sauce
½ c. pork butt or rib shavings

1. Combine all ingredients. Cook on top of stove in cast iron pot.
2. Cook on low heat for 2-3 hours.

Serves: 12-15
Preparation: 10 minutes
Cooking: 2-3 hours

"We reduced this down from 5 cases of beans... you'll love the down-home flavor."

— NOTES —

BARBECUED RIBS A LA JUNCTION
(Make Sauce Ahead — Start Grill)

4-6	lbs. loin pork or beef ribs
1	c. Hunt's ketchup
1	c. tomato sauce (Theresa's, if available)
½	c. water
1	T. soy sauce
2	T. Worcestershire sauce
2	T. prepared mustard
½	t. powdered garlic
	tabasco to taste
¼	c. beer (warm, domestic)
	Option: cayenne pepper, homegrown peppers

— RIBS —

1. Place ribs on rack over barbecue pit 2 feet above heat so they won't char. Make certain the coals are very hot.
2. Turn ribs frequently to keep juices inside. Cook for approximately 45 minutes.

— SAUCE —

3. Combine all ingredients except beer. Mix in warm beer, just enough to percolate all ingredients.
4. Cook the sauce until hot over medium heat. Stir well.
5. Baste ribs with sauce last 15 minutes or add sauce after barbecuing.

VARIATIONS: To make a great hot sauce, add cayenne pepper and several types of home grown peppers.

Serves: 4-6
Preparation: 10 minutes
Cooking: 45 minutes

"One of the tastiest barbecue sauces you'll ever taste!"

Jack's Skyway Restaurant, St. Petersburg, Florida

Jack's Skyway Restaurant

— St. Petersburg —

Jack Thomas learned how to do an egg justice while briefly assigned as a mess cook in the Navy. He now shares his breakfast favorites with hundreds of civilians each morning to the tune of 2,500 eggs, 400 pounds of potatoes, 1,000 biscuits, 100 pounds of sausage, 45 pounds of bacon and 4,000 cups of coffee each week.

His career as a short-order cook was interrupted by studies to attain his University of Florida graduate degree and 17 years as an engineer for Tampa Electric. Tiring of the grind, he took early retirement in 1976. That lasted only a month when a relative suggested he take over the restaurant located in the late Hap O'Neill's Skyway Boat Basin, a 5.6-acre marina/fish camp located at the north end of the Skyway Bridge.

Jack had enjoyed doing fish fries and barbecues for community events in Brandon and thought his cumulative experience in volume cooking could be applied here. He and his wife, Carol, spent several months remodeling the restaurant. Together they developed recipes for their breakfast-only menu.

Skyway Jack's was an immediate success, serving primarily

to local fishermen. It wasn't long before area professionals joined them.

He serves them all eggs cooked in eight different ways, plus a variety of omelets, including the Tex-Cheese filled with chili and cheese. Eggs can be teamed up with sausage, steaks, country ham, bacon or fried fish. Jack also serves blueberry or his famous banana pancakes and pecan waffles.

But what has made him an international breakfast king —' he has been written up in three London newspapers and receives Canadian raves as well — are his one-of-a-kind specials: Philadelphia-style Scrapple (made with a hog's head and feet, pork liver and pork roast), Baked Apples, Ham What-am, Old Navy Breakfast (baked beans, sausage and cornbread), Southern Breakfast featuring pork chops, and Jack's trademark, S.O.S., which is creamed sausage on biscuits. Breakfasts are served with home-fried potatoes or grits and a choice of homemade biscuits or toast, which is really no choice as you're missing out on a real treat if you don't go for the biscuits.

Jack opens for breakfast well before sunrise, and if you go on a weekend, that's when you'll have to be there to avoid a wait. The restaurant seats fewer than 50 people, and somewhere around 500 are served on a typical Sunday morning.

A few years ago Jack extended his hours to include a lunch menu, and, because you can't stop a good thing, he further extended them to the early evening.

The two best-sellers on the sandwich list are the Sloppy Jack and Carol's Fishburger. Smoked and Old Country Ham are the dinner favorites. Every three months a new recipe invented by either Carol or Jack is added to the menu.

The decor of Jack's Skyway is, well, eclectic Skyway. There's something of a nautical look with porthole windows, life rings, and pilings and moorings on the outside. The restrooms are labeled "Heads" and the kitchen "Galley." But the ship's theme ends there, with dozens of plaques graphically depicting the menu choices, a two-foot Buddha precariously dangling over the grill, and several plaques lettered with Jack's life philosophies.

The atmosphere is apparently too hard to duplicate. Though he opened another restaurant at 1247 1st Avenue North, St. Petersburg, called Skyway Jack's, with identical menu and quality of food, he says it isn't the same without the water and unique characters of the marina around the corner.

Try it — for local color in St. Pete, Jack's Skyway is practically an institution!

How to get there: *6701 34th Street South, St. Petersburg. Take Interstate 275 or U.S. Highway 19 to the north end of the Skyway Bridge. The restaurant is one-fourth of a mile north of the Toll Plaza.*

While you're here: *You are just a few miles from one of Florida's favorite recreational areas, Fort DeSoto Park on Mullet Key. The park, which is actually several islands, offers camping, picnic grounds, beaches, fishing piers, and a boat launch area. It is also the site of the old fort that once protected Tampa Harbor from Spanish invasion.*

Also, the Boyd Hill Nature Trail on Lake Maggiore, located at 9th Street and Country Club Way South, takes visitors through natural ecosystems by way of boardwalks and trails.

The Haas Museum, located at 3511 2nd Avenue South, is several century-old homes authentically refurnished with artifacts, clothing, tools and furniture belonging to local pioneer families. Guides take guests through the homes explaining how the artifacts were used and telling interesting stories about the early settlers.

SLOPPY JACKS

1	lb. ground beef (or ground chuck)
½	c. onion (minced)
¼	c. celery (minced)
⅔	c. green pepper (minced)
1	c. catsup
¼	c. water
1	T. liquid mustard
¼	t. salt
¼	t. garlic powder
½	t. pepper
2	c. finely shredded cabbage (⅛-³⁄₁₆" thick)

1. Cook ground beef (or chuck) in large skillet. Break apart until fine and crumbly. Drain grease.
2. Add all other ingredients, except cabbage. Mix thoroughly. Bring to boil.
3. Add cabbage. Mix thoroughly. Simmer with lid for 25 minutes. Stir frequently.
4. If extra has been made, portion out and freeze.* Serve the remaining in bakery buns and enjoy!

   *Note: If available, best to use microwave oven to heat the frozen portions — will not dry them out.

Serves: 4-5
Preparation: 15 minutes
Cooking: 35 minutes

"A most unusual nutritious and different lunch dish, especially for growing Jacks of all ages!"

— NOTES —

JACK'S CHILI

1	lb. lean ground beef (or ground chuck)
¾	c. tomato juice
1	15 oz. can whole tomatoes (crush with hand)
1	15 oz. can dark red kidney beans
¼	c. onions (diced)
⅓	c. celery (diced)
1	t. Worcestershire sauce
1½	T. chili powder
⅓	T. garlic powder
⅓	t. pepper
½	t. salt
½	t. cumin
	Optional: tabasco

1. Cook meat over medium heat until brown and crumbly.
2. Remove from heat. Drain grease. Add all the remaining ingredients. Mix thoroughly.
3. Return to heat and bring to boil, stirring constantly. Lower heat and simmer for 3 hours, covered. Stir occasionally.
4. Tabasco can be added if "hot" is desired.
5. Any extra can be frozen if cooled first.

Serves: 4
Preparation: 15 minutes
Cooking: 3 hours 15 minutes

"A very satisfying dish!"

— NOTES —

JACK'S SKYWAY RESTAURANT
ST. PETERSBURG

JACK'S S.O.S.
(Creamed Sausage on Biscuits)

2	T. vegetable oil
½	lb. spicy sausage meat (can use mild or hot)
¾	c. all-purpose flour
1	qt. milk
¾	t. salt
	pepper and sage to taste

1. Heat oil in 2-quart saucepan. Add sausage in small pieces. Cook on medium heat with lid.
2. As meat cooks, break up into crumbly texture while stirring several times. Cook until dark brown. (Do not drain)
3. Add flour — a little at a time — thoroughly mixing after each addition. Cook and stir frequently for 6-10 minutes.
4. Meanwhile, in another saucepan, heat milk and salt until just starting to boil.
5. Add hot milk to sausage mixture, a little at a time, while stirring constantly with wire whisk.
6. Allow to thicken for 5-8 minutes. Taste and add desired seasonings.
7. Serve over biscuits or toast points.

Serves: 4
Preparation: 5 minutes
Cooking: 20-25 minutes

"An old southern favorite that is always good!"

— NOTES —

CAROL'S FISHBURGERS

2-2½ lbs. boneless and skinless fish
3   c. water
1   T. salt
¼   c. onion (minced)
¼   c. celery (minced)
¼   c. green pepper (minced)
½   c. mashed potatoes
1   egg (beaten)
¾   t. Worcestershire sauce
⅛   t. garlic powder
½   T. MSG
½-⅓ c. breading mix
     oil for frying
     bakery buns

1. Bring fish to boil in salted water. Simmer only 10 minutes. Drain off water just until fish is slightly moist.
2. Crumble fish. Mix with other ingredients. Use enough breading mix to hold ingredients together.
3. Make into patties, using about 4 oz. per patty, each about 4" in size and ⅜-½" thick.
4. If more have been made than are needed, freeze between sheets of waxed paper.
5. Lay the remaining patties on cookie sheet or similar tray. Freeze several hours until frozen.
6. Deep fat fry frozen patties until golden brown in oil heated to 350°F.
7. Drain on paper towels. Serve on bun with tartar sauce. (See recipe on page 87)

Serves: 5
Preparation: 15 minutes
Cooking: 10 minutes
Freeze: 2-3 hours

"Make up a batch to freeze and have on hand for when needed!"

— NOTES —

El Cap Inn

— St. Petersburg —

Many of us are borderline hamburger gourmets. We're old enough to remember what a good hamburger should taste like and young enough to have been solidly media programmed to pull into one of the fast-food dispensaries whenever our tummies call for a burger and fries.

Many St. Petersburg locals bill the El Cap hamburger as one of the best burgers on the Suncoast. Here you will rediscover the burger of your youth.

What can make a hamburger different? In this case, the answer is who. It's Frank and Mary Jean Bonfili, and their "one and only" waitress, Beverly. Frank and Mary Jean took over the ownership and management of El Cap in 1980 from Frank's parents, Steve and Rose Bonfili, who founded the Inn in 1963.

Nothing has been changed, not the quality of the food, the recipes, the menu, the decor, the atmosphere, the clientele... not even Beverly, who has provided both the service and entertainment for El Cap's for the past 19 years. All right, the prices *have* changed. But you can still get one of the best burgers in town for under a dollar.

While Mary Jean handles all the food preparation for the eight-item menu and variations on the same themes, Frank handles the beer and wine bar, referees baseball debates (usually settled by "The Library," an enormous collection of baseball resource materials occupying a large cabinet behind the bar), and converses with the regulars who have made El Cap their home.

Meanwhile, Beverly literally races about collecting and delivering orders to a full house including a modest outdoor courtyard. Beverly truly makes the place, as well as puts customers *in* their place. She treats everyone as if she's known them forever; many she has. She's a rough 'n' tough lady but dearly loved by all, proof being that not once in her years at El Cap's has anyone ever walked out on a bill.

"They wouldn't get a block away from here without me grabbing 'em," she says, with more conviction than you usually hear from a woman over 60. Her spunk and vigor are a result of her "go power," the java she slugs down like shots of whiskey, according to Mary Jean.

The decor is part baseball, part everything else. Frank's uncle, Augie Donatelli, was a famous umpire for the National League. And, as Uncle Hugo was both a baseball player and a boxer, memorabilia of both sports flank the walls. St. Pete's spring training season fills El Cap's with Minor League players, local softball teams, and spectators of each. Frank says El Cap's is feeding its third generation of baseball enthusiasts. Lunch hour also brings in a good number of downtown professionals. They provide an interesting but harmonious contrast to the local color.

El Cap's not only makes you feel at home, Frank and Mary Jean allow you to make it home. At least half the decor is memorabilia, trinkets, plaques, pennants and pictures brought in by regulars to make at least a small part of the Inn their own.

With more than a million burgers served since El Cap Inn opened, you would think the personal touch would be impossible to achieve. But, as one regular says, "If Frank doesn't say hello to you by name when you come in, it means it's your first visit to El Cap's."

And your first visit won't be your last.

How to get there: 3500-4th Street North, St. Petersburg. From I-275 heading south, take the 38th Avenue North exit. Turn left to 4th Street, then right to 35th Avenue North. Never open on Sundays. Closed for R&R, and top-to-bottom cleaning, the month of August.

While you're here: Visit Sunken Gardens, a menagerie of Florida foliage, flowers, birds and reptiles in a beautiful, natural setting. A huge walk-through aviary features more than 350 birds to entertain and educate your entire family.

THE EL CAP BURGER

1	lb. ground chuck (from corn-fed steer)
4	"good buns" (homemade or from bakery)
	salt and freshly ground black pepper
4	process cheese slices
4	large Ruskin* tomato slices (or other kind of hearty tomato)
4	Bermuda onion slices (*largest* you can find)
4	crisp, fresh lettuce leaves
	homemade ketchup
	*Great Florida tomatoes!

1. Hand-pack patties (4 to pound). Chill until firm.
2. Use an old, well seasoned grill or electric frying pan (the oldness and seasoned surface are the secrets to cloning their burger). If you have a dual heat control grill, heat one side to 385 °F for the buns and the other side to 340 °F for the patties.
3. Place fresh patties on grill and cook partially. Do not press down. Turn over, salt and pepper second side. Cook until medium rare.
4. Top with cheese slices, remove and place on bottom of grilled bun. Add tomato and onion slices and lettuce. Follow with top of grilled bun.

Variations: Add your favorite seasonings, if desired.

Serves: 4
Preparation: 15 minutes
Cooking: 5 minutes

"The finest ingredients make the finest meals!"

— NOTES —

CHICKEN CACCIATORA

4	T. butter
5	T. lard
2	whole cloves garlic (crushed)
4	chicken breast halves (or other chicken pieces)
½	c. sherry
	pinch sage
	salt and pepper to taste
2	*Finger Hot* peppers (cut in half lengthwise, remove seeds)
2	*Hung Waxed* peppers (cut in half lengthwise, remove seeds)
½	c. fresh parsley (chopped)

1. Melt butter and lard in large skillet. Add garlic. Dry chicken pieces with paper towels. Add to skillet.
2. Brown on each side. Add sherry. Turn heat down and place half of each type of pepper on each chicken piece.
3. Cover and simmer for 20-30 minutes.
4. Remove lid, cover top with fresh parsley and simmer for another 5-10 minutes.
5. Serve with white rice and fresh Italian bread to dip into sauce.

NOTE: IMMEDIATELY after handling the fresh peppers, wash hands with plenty of soap and water and do not touch hands to face, especially eyes.

According to Mary Jean, this is a great dish to create after preparing hundreds of hamburgers a day for their customers. This is an old family recipe and is served in the Bonfili home twice a week.

Serves: 4
Preparation: 10 minutes
Cooking: 30-45 minutes

"Spicy hot without having a sauce spooned over. Unusual!"

— NOTES —

— NOTES —

Chris' Restaurant

— Fort Pierce —

Chris' Restaurant, on North U.S. 1 in Fort Pierce, is the type of diner that has inspired novelists, playwrights, script-writers and songwriters to themes of nostalgia with the diner taking the lead role.

It is a no-frills place that offers a square, balanced, home-cooked meal at a low price. It is the kind of place where the owner waves hello to customers and waitresses take personal responsibility for your satisfaction.

Not only is the restaurant inspirational for script themes, the owner, Hercules P. Christ (Chris), has a life story that would lend itself to a best-seller.

Chris spent his childhood on the Greek island of Cyprus on the east side of the Mediterranean Sea, off the coast of Syria. He was born Hercules Christodoulou, which means strength and slave of Christ. At age 9, he left his family and his island for the mainland to get work in order to raise money to come to the United States. A teacher in Cyprus had told him about the U.S., and at that young age Chris developed a passion to live here. He got jobs on merchant ships and tried several times to come to this country, once as a stow-away, always to be returned for the lack of proper visas and entry papers.

In between attempts to enter the U.S., he would find jobs in restaurants while traveling through Europe, Egypt and India. The bulk of his culinary talents he credits to his experience at the King George Hotel in Port Said, Egypt, and nine years with acclaimed European chefs.

His final attempt to enter the U.S., in 1948, was well-planned. Chris had spent years studying maps of New York City, memorizing street names and locations of places he would need to find. Since he spoke no English, he didn't want to draw attention to himself by asking. He had learned from experience that in order to secure his safety, he would have to get out of New York, where immigrants were scrutinized, as soon as possible.

He arrived in November wearing only shorts, shirt and sandals, not even a coat. At the bus station his plan was to stand behind someone buying a ticket and simply to say "same" when it came his turn. It was one of the few words he had learned. He had only $17, and the ticket to Ohio cost nearly that much.

A miracle awaited him when he stepped off the bus into an unfamiliar town and state. Across the street was a Greek Restaurant...and not only did the owner speak Chris' language, but gave him a job.

He spent the next 17 years there working and taking classes to prepare for his granted citizenship, a long-awaited dream come true. He married and had four daughters. In 1965 he came to Fort Pierce on vacation and decided to make it a permanent move, opening a restaurant on Second Street and later moving to his present location.

Chris' lifetime experience in the restaurant business, as well as the variety of his personal experience, shows in his cooking, and the menu. With nearly 75 entree choices on the lunch and dinner menus, you can choose from seafood, Italian, meat, poultry and vegetarian dinners. You can also enjoy fabulous breakfasts that barely budge the budget.

Oddly enough, though he has vast amounts of ethnic cooking experience, it's obvious that he favors down-home American country cooking...though, considering he spent half his life trying to become an American, that should come as no surprise.

Chris' best seller is his liver and onion dinner. He cooks up nearly 200 orders a day, 400 pounds a week — and has prepared this dish for 38 years. He buys the liver unsliced, freezes it, lets it slightly thaw, slices it paper thin (much thinner than the supermarket butcher), and removes all the "skin" and veins. It is cooked just 30 seconds on each side and melts in your mouth! Added to the meal is a bowl of potato soup made from scratch, mashed potatoes and homemade gravy and fresh green beans. Top it off with rice pudding.

Chris is very conscious of nutrition in his food preparation, so much so that local doctors prescribe at least a few meals a week at his restaurant to their elderly patients, which aside from nutrition, offers prices they can afford.

The dedication to hard work, a desire for perfection in all things, and zest for good and abundant eating characterizing the Greek ethic, are evident in this restaurant. Other than this, Chris is as American as apple pie, and proud of it.

How to get there: 901 North U.S. 1. Take the Florida Turnpike or Interstate 95 to the S.R. 68 exit. Head east into Fort Pierce to U.S. 1. Turn left to address. Closed on holidays.

While you're here: The area is filled with beautiful, natural park areas. The Jack Island Preserve on A1A allows only foot traffic on the Island and is considered one of the finest natural plant and wildlife sanctuaries in the state. You should also visit Pepper State Park on North A1A and The Savannahs at 200 Midway Road, off U.S. 1. It's 550 acres of gardens, camping, swimming and fresh-water fishing.

POTATO SOUP

3	large white potatoes (peeled, cooked, diced)
1	stalk celery (diced)
1	carrot (diced)
½	small onion (diced)
1	T. pimiento
1	qt. milk
	salt and pepper to taste
½	c. fresh or frozen peas
¼	c. + 2 T. flour
¼	c. water

1. Combine first six ingredients plus salt and pepper in large pot.
2. Cover. Simmer over low heat until vegetables are tender.
3. Approximately one-half hour prior to serving, add peas.
4. 5 minutes prior to serving, mix flour and water together to make a paste. Add to soup. Cook until thickened. Stir several times.

Serves: 6
Preparation: 20 minutes
Cooking: 45 minutes to 1 hour

"Great for a chilly night — warms you throughout!"

— NOTES —

CHRIS' SPECIALTY — LIVER AND ONIONS
(Freeze Liver Ahead)

1   **lb. baby beef liver or calves liver (in slices)**
½   **c. flour**
     vegetable oil (for frying)
2   **large onions (sliced thin)**
¼   **c. butter**

1. Freeze slices of liver singly. Thaw until hard but sliceable.
2. Cut in very, very thin slices (less than ¼ " thick) (devein and skin slices if necessary)
3. Gently dip into flour to seal juices.
4. Saute onions slowly, in butter, until almost transparent.
5. Heat thin layer of vegetable oil in another skillet to 350 °F.
6. Add floured liver to heated oil. Cook for **only** ½ minute on each side.
7. Serve liver with the sauteed onions.

Serves: 4
Preparation: Several hours to freeze liver plus
                20 minutes
Cooking: 15 minutes

"The secret to delicious liver is the short hot cooking — It's delicious!"

— NOTES —

RICE PUDDING

1   **c. long grain white rice**
2   **c. water**
½   **t. salt**
2   **c. milk**
1   **c. sugar**
2   **large eggs**
¼   **t. cinnamon**
Optional: Raisins

1. Combine rice, water, and salt in pan. Bring to boil. Simmer until tender and dry.
2. Add 1½ cups milk. Add sugar to rice.
3. Combine other ½ cup milk and eggs. Beat until smooth.
4. Temper egg mixture by adding a small amount of warmed milk from rice pan to bowl. (Bring eggs up to very warm temperature while stirring them.)
5. Slowly, and stirring constantly, pour tempered egg mixture back into rice pan. Cook over low heat until thick.
6. Add cinnamon.

Serves: 8
Preparation: 5 minutes
Cooking: 30 minutes

"Like momma used to make!! A thick pudding and excellent!"

— NOTES —

— NOTES —

The Desert Inn, Yeehaw Junction, Florida

The Desert Inn

— Yeehaw Junction —

Anyone who has done any traveling in this state has driven by The Desert Inn. Many of you have been by it so many times, you probably don't even see it anymore. The restaurant is like its home, Yeehaw Junction...you *have* to drive by, but you never plan to stop there.

The Desert Inn is probably the only restaurant in the state that is responsible for single-handedly creating and naming a community. Built more than 50 years ago, it's the second oldest restaurant in this book. Though run by Jackie and Bill Mc-Carthy for eight years, it is still part of its originator's estate, Alfred Cheverette. It was built at the crossroads of Highways 441 and 60, which once served a a station of the Florida East Coast Railroad. Because of the donkeys in the backyard of the restaurant, people began calling it Jackass Junction.

When the turnpike was built and the state government was forced to put it on the map as an interchange, officials wanted to rename it Crossroads. The community, which is not a city or a township and therefore has no government, fought the state. They finally settled the dispute by saying the state could call it anything they wanted, but the community would continue to call it Jackass Junction. The apparent compromise was Yeehaw Junction, though locals and truckers haven't yet compromised.

Bill and Jackie reluctantly came to the Desert Inn Motel and Restaurant after Bill had discovered it on his sales territory. Bill agreed to run the place for Mr. Cheverette when he became ill. That was eight years ago and now Bill and Jackie are as much a part of this landmark as the building itself. The Desert Inn has remained a landmark not only for its antiquity, but also for the quality of its home-cooked food. Breakfast, lunch and dinner, seven days a week, the restaurant is filled with local diners, truckers and adventurous tourists who often don't realize when they get off the turnpike here, that there isn't much to get off to.

I say adventurous because the Desert Inn's exterior isn't particularly inviting. The neon sign blasts "GOOD FOOD" in three-foot letters to passers-by, but the building — not altered a bit in fifty years, right down to the gas pumps — doesn't exactly say the same thing. Jackie says that quite often a family will drive up and send the father in on a reconnaissance mission. When satisfied, he hails the rest of his troops.

The inside, however, is just fine. Seating 65 (63 if you eliminate the two chairs occupied by two life-size and life-like wooden Indians that are permanent customers) at tables, booths, and the bar, the restaurant is clean, homey and comfortable.

The menu is typical of an old-time diner with a little bit of everything to satisfy all types, and they do see all types here. Roast Beef and Old Fashion Dressing, Meatloaf, Pork Chops, several Steaks, Southern Fried Chicken, Catfish and Hushpuppies (the most popular), Shrimp, Scallops and Oysters, and Frog Legs are featured.

The food is all homemade, right down to the chili and chowders, the doughnuts (made with an ice cream scoop), and the sausage that Bill makes himself. His father had been a butcher and taught him how to do it right. He buys a whole pig and half of a steer and makes up 500 pounds at a time! He also makes up a batch from wild boar and venison, but that's *his* private stock.

The Desert Inn also benefits from having the only package liquor license in the area. Bill says it's as old as the Inn itself but worth five times as much. The off-sale shop, actually more like the old-time bank windows with bars, looks just like it did in the 1930s. Some of those bottles are probably aged more than their labels claim.

The back room is the Trucker's Lounge, with a separate door and a buzzer for placing orders. It was originally designed for the days when segregation was enforced, and Jackie says that not long ago, a government representative paid a "friendly" visit to see if it was still used for that purpose.

Beyond the historical and food values of the Desert Inn, what really makes the visit worthwhile are Bill and Jackie's zany personalities. As living proof that life can be fun after 50, these two may remind you of a George Burns and Gracie Allen routine, though Jackie has more cranium substance, in that they are always battling for the better laugh. Were Vaudeville still around, these two could make top billing in slapstick comedy. I hesitate to go into descriptions of all their pranks, for fear of spoiling your (and their) fun. After being the victim of a few, I was prompted to ask how many customers had not returned.

"Oh, we lose a couple now and then," Bill says. "But it's worth the laugh!"

The entire restaurant is a fun house straight out of a circus. Part of the fun is watching Bill and Jackie compete for first place in performance. Their repertoire of jokes is endless. I wish I could tell you all the things they pulled from their "goody bag," but it would defeat the purpose as much as telling you the ending of a good movie that you should see for yourself. Just tell Bill and Jackie that we sent you, and then "go with the flow." The entertainment here is excellent, and there's no cover charge! It's as hilarious as a laugh box...oops, I gave one away.

How to get there: If you are doing any cross-state traveling, chances are it's on your way. It's located off the Florida Turnpike at the intersection of Highways 441 and 60, 23 miles west of Vero Beach, in Yeehaw Junction.

While you're here: This is it, folks. If you have friends on the opposite coast, this is a central location to meet them. You might want to steal an idea from a couple who frequents the restaurant and once invited another couple to join them. They led them to believe that they were going to a fancy dinner club and had them dress up in their best. If your friends are good sports, it will be a night to remember. Call Bill and Jackie ahead of time so they will put on their best performance.

POTATO SALAD

3	lbs. potatoes
2½	c. mayonnaise
¾	c. dill pickle relish
¼	c. pimiento
¼	c. onion (chopped)
¼	c. prepared mustard (brown will give a tasty zing) salt and pepper to taste
1	dozen cooked eggs (chopped)

1. Peel potatoes. Boil whole until done. Cool.
2. Cut into 1¼ " chunks. Place in large bowl.
3. Mix together all remaining ingredients except eggs. Stir into potatoes.
4. Add eggs to potatoes and mix gently. Chill until ready to serve.

Serves: 8-10
Preparation: 20 minutes
Cooking: 30 minutes
Chill: 2-4 hours

"Simple but more flavorful than most!"

— NOTES —

DESERT INN MEATLOAF

2	lbs. hamburger (best to use ground chuck or round)
2	eggs
2	hamburger buns (broken into small pieces)
½	c. onion (diced)
½	c. green pepper (diced)
¼	c. catsup
¼	c. sugar
	several dashes tabasco sauce
¼	c. yellow cornmeal
½	c. grated cheddar cheese
	salt and pepper to taste

1. In large mixing bowl, break apart meat. Add all remaining ingredients.
2. Using clean hands (minus any jewelry) squish all ingredients together until well mixed.
3. Form into loaf shape and place in 8 x 10″ baking dish.
4. Bake in 300°F oven for 1-1½ hours, until done.

Serves: 8
Preparation: 15 minutes
Cooking: 1-1½ hours

"Catsup and sugar blend together beautifully to form a glaze-like mixture. Your mouth will water for weeks."

— NOTES —

DESERT INN PECAN PIE

6 **eggs**
1 **c. sugar**
2 **T. melted butter**
2 **t. vanilla**
1 **T. flour**
1½ **c. maple syrup**
9½ -10″ deep dish unbaked pie shell
   whole pecan halves

1. Whip eggs. Add sugar, mix well.
2. Add butter, vanilla, flour and maple syrup, blending well and until smooth.
3. Pour into pie shell. Place pecans in single layer in a circular pattern across top.
4. Bake at 400°F for an additional 40 minutes.

Serves: 8
Preparation: 15 minutes
Cooking: 50 minutes

"Unusual variation, not as overbearingly rich as most pecan pies."

— NOTES —

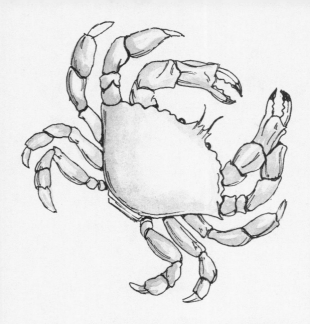

The Crab Trap

— Palmetto —

"Something old, something new, something borrowed, something blue" may originally have been written for wedding bliss, but it also describes The Crab Trap in Palmetto.

Lee and Margaret Cline, owners of this award-winning restaurant, have incorporated several old Maryland recipes for seafood (something old), influenced by their previous residence in the Chesapeake Bay area. Many of these recipes are for the Bay's Blue Crab (something blue), for which The Crap Trap received its fame. Two shipments of fresh Maryland Blue Crabs come in each week.

The Clines are continually testing their gourmet fantasies, first in their own kitchen and then on their customers. An insert in the menu is specially designed for the "idea-of-the-week," and customers are asked to give their candid opinions on making the dish a permanent menu item (something new).

What gives the menu its distinctive character are the dishes "borrowed" from the Clines' world travels. Caribbean and European influences are obvious in the titles given to several of the items, as well as a number of Deep South and Florida Cracker dishes.

"What it comes down to," says Lee, "is, if it's different, we'll put it on the menu."

Florida Alligator, Black Tip Shark, Soft Turtle Cooter, Wild Boar in Red Sauce, Sword Fish Steak, Florida Perch, Frog Legs, Caribbean Turtle made with mushrooms and onions, Chicken Baltimore, Barbecued Shrimp and Fillet of Scamp (the cadillac of the grouper family) are a few of the dishes that set The Crab Trap apart from other seafood restaurants.

If you're an oyster lover, try the Oysters Parisian. Baked in the half-shell with sour cream and a rich Parmesan/butter topping, they are scrumptious!

If you stop for lunch, try the Antipasto Sandwich, recently introduced. Ham, salami, olives, onions and peppers are chopped and mixed with a mayonnaise dressing, plentifully heaped on between two slices of bread with cheese, grilled, and topped with lettuce and tomato.

For side dishes, consider Crab Critter Fritters, Onion Kurls, or Scalloped Bananas, breaded and fried banana chunks, deep fried, and rolled in sugar and cinnamon.

All of the dishes, right down to the crab cakes (which have just an ounce of crackers to a pound of meat) and salad dressings, are prepared from scratch and to order. Even the most common dishes have a special "Crab Trap" touch, such as basting the fish fillets in mayonnaise before frying or broiling to seal in the flavor.

Lee and Margaret established their reputation in their first Palmetto restaurant called The Sea Hut, which opened in 1971. Following six months of Lee's unsuccessful retirement, he says due to an aversion to golf, he and Carol purchased The Crab Trap.

Lee himself made all of the light fixtures, created from fish traps and a design based on hanging planters. The ceilings are covered with various types of woven grass and reeds, the walls decorated in cedar with cypress knees and fans. The spacious booths, a favorite among regulars, have raised, cork-covered backs for acoustical purposes. Colorful, hand-crafted exotic birds ordered from St. Croix add a tropical flavor and are also a big seller.

No matter what day of the week or time of day, the parking lot in front of the restaurant is filled to capacity. With only 76 seats in the dining room, you're likely to have a wait, but you will be comfortably accommodated in an over-sized lounge area designed for just that purpose. As Lee says, "I can serve lousy food quickly or exceptional food slowly." For the tasty experience The Crap Trap offers, your wait will be well rewarded.

How to get there: The restaurant is located two miles south of the Skyway Bridge south toll plaza on Highway 19 in Palmetto, just north of Sarasota-Bradenton. It is open daily for lunch and dinner.

While you're here: The Gamble Mansion on U.S. 301 in Ellenton, just ten minutes from the restaurant, is the oldest building on Florida's west coast. The guided tours of this typical example of antebellum architecture allow guests to experience the romance of the Old South. There are also picnic grounds on the premises.

CRAB TRAP FRITTERS

½   lb. blue crab meat (preferably fresh)
1   egg
¼   c. milk
1   c. all purpose biscuit mix
     juice of whole lemon
⅛   t. garlic salt
¼   t. salt
½   t. parsley flakes
6   drops Worcestershire sauce
     vegetable oil

1.   **Carefully** remove all cartilage from crab meat.
2.   In a bowl beat egg. Add milk and stir in biscuit mix.
3.   Add seasonings and crab meat. Mix gently.
     Set aside.
4.   In a very heavy skillet, heat 2 or 3 inches of oil to
     375°F.
5.   Drop batter into hot oil by half teaspoonsful.
     Fry until golden brown.

Serves: 4-6
Preparation: 10 minutes
Cooking: 5-10 minutes

"Great with tartar sauce or cocktail sauce!"

— NOTES —

CRAB TRAP CRAB CREPES

— CREPE BATTER —

¾	c. sifted flour
½	t. salt
2	eggs (beaten)
1	c. milk
1	t. melted butter

— CREPE FILLING —

2	T. butter
2	T. flour
½	t. tabasco sauce
¼	t. Worcestershire sauce
½	t. dry mustard
½	t. salt
1	c. evaporated milk
2	T. Parmesan cheese
1	T. cream sherry wine
12	oz. blue crab meat (preferably fresh)

— CREPE BATTER —

1. Combine flour, salt, eggs and milk. Blend until smooth.
2. To mixture add melted butter and blend. Let stand several hours.
3. Heat a 5″ skillet. Using about 2 tablespoons crepe batter for each crepe, spread evenly by tilting pan. Brown crepe.
4. As each crepe is done, place in separate pan. Cover to keep warm.

— FILLING —

5. Melt butter. Add flour, tabasco, Worcestershire, mustard and salt. Blend slowly. Add evaporated milk. Stir until thick.
6. Remove from heat. Stir in Parmesan and cream sherry to make crepe sauce.

7. Add ¼ cup of crepe sauce to the crab meat (be sure to remove all cartilage) and mix.
8. Place 3 tablespoons or 1½ oz. of crab meat mixture into crepe. Gently roll up.
9. Place rolled crepe in shallow baking dish. Thin remaining sauce and gently spoon over crepes. Bake at 400°F for 10-12 minutes.

Serves: 4-6
Preparation: 2-3 hours for crepes to set
Cooking: 15 minutes crepes/20 minutes filling

"A very easy-no-fail recipe!"

— NOTES —

CHICKEN BALTIMORE

4	chicken breast halves (de-boned)
4	T. butter
	salt and pepper to taste
8	scalloped bananas (See recipe on page 65)
4	peach halves and juice

1. Saute chicken breasts in butter, salt, and pepper until tender and browned.
2. Serve each with 2 scalloped bananas alongside and a peach half and juice on top.

Serves: 4
Preparation: 10 minutes
Cooking: 15-20 minutes

"Pretty as a picture!"

— NOTES —

OYSTERS PARISIAN

½   c. butter
1   c. Parmesan cheese
½   c. cracker crumbs
1   t. dry mustard
    whole oysters (quantity depends on number
    to serve)
    sour cream

1.   Soften butter. Combine cheese, crumbs and
     mustard.
2.   Form into roll approximately 2½" in diameter. Roll
     in waxed paper and chill until firm.
3.   Shuck oysters. Leave in half shell. Top each with
     1 t. sour cream and slice of Parmesan/butter roll.
4.   Bake in 350°F oven until golden brown, about
     10-12 minutes.

Serves: you decide
Preparation: 1 hour 25 minutes
Cooking: 15 minutes

*"What could be easier if oysters are shucked ahead
of time!"*

— NOTES —

SCALLOPED BANANAS

4 **medium ripe bananas**
1 **c. flour**
½ **c. milk**
1 **c. bread crumbs (unseasoned)**
 oil for frying
⅓ **c. cinnamon/sugar mixture (equal mix)**

1. Cut bananas into 3-4 1¾" chunks.
2. Roll each chunk in flour. Dip in milk, then roll in bread crumbs.
3. Deep fat fry in oil heated to 350°F until golden.
4. Roll in cinnamon/sugar mixture. Serve warm.

Serves: 4-6
Preparation: 10 minutes
Cooking: 5 minutes

"Can be served as a side dish with meal or as a dessert. Either way is sure to please!"

— NOTES —

— NOTES —

Old Towne Cafe

"It takes just three things to be served here . . . courtesy, patience and money."
— Bill Berring, owner, Old Towne Cafe

— Naples —

Naples would be a fascinating thesis topic for a student seeking a master's degree in urban planning and development. It is both the richest and poorest of communities in Florida. Though per capita wealth ranks high, it is distributed unevenly.

The Old Towne Cafe is an obscure restaurant that attempts to bridge this gap between the echelons of society in this unusual, albeit beautiful, community.

Owner Bill Berring has considerable experience in the gourmet restaurant business, with 25 years in haute cuisine for several nationally famous restaurants such as the Greenbrier in White Sulfur Springs, West Virginia; the Boca Raton Resort Hotel and Club, on the Gold Coast; South Seas Plantation, on Captiva Island; and most recently, the Shore Club in Naples. He has also traveled and worked for restaurants in Europe.

When the Shore Club found and recruited him to Florida, he discovered a void in the restaurant business that needed to be filled.

"There is an entire community within a community here that works in the fancy restaurants and lounges. There was nothing to do, and nowhere for these people to go when they got off work at two or three in the morning," he says. "Just like people who work eight-to-five don't go straight home and to bed, neither do we."

So in the fall of 1980 with the help of many friends who donated time, and some of the local restaurants who supported his idea, Bill opened the Old Towne Cafe. Named for its proximity to Naples Old Town section, which is actually very new, it is open through the night from 10 p.m. until 2 p.m. the next day, serving a limited but top quality menu of egg dishes and more than a dozen sandwiches prepared to order.

At first, because of the location, off the main strip with no signs or lighting, no one knew it was there. The restaurant has since moved to a more visible spot. Bill says only pride kept him going through the first year, and credits his wife with turning the tables on the restaurant's success.

"Suzanne came down to help me one morning, though there was no one in the place. So at 4:30 in the morning, she went out and stood in the middle of Hwy. 41 with a sign pointing to the Cafe, with big letters saying "OPEN." A local disc jockey was on her way to work when the sign aroused her curiosity. She came in, ate, and has been plugging our place on her show ever since."

That was just what the place needed. The quality was already there. Now Bill has no trouble filling his open-kitchen, casual cafe. He says his customers come in shifts. First around 2 a.m., the waiters, waitresses, and bartenders come in. Then the local restaurant clean-up people around 3 or 4 a.m. Then the fishermen on their way out to work, or pleasure. Between them are all the local firemen, police officers, and emergency squads. An unintentional but most welcome ingredient in this melting pot are the high society types who have been to one of the entertainment establishments in the area who want a bite to eat before heading home. In the morning, Old Towne Cafe serves breakfast to the 8-to-5'ers. And on the weekends, families are in the majority.

Around 2 a.m. is the busiest and most lively time. Bill says he knows most of the people who come in and the atmosphere is more like having a party in his own home. Some come back to give him a hand. Many are standing against the wall, plate in hand. In the winter, they gather around the stove for warmth.

"Because the bulk of my customers are those in the business, I am cooking for the fussiest clientele possible," Bill says.

But he lives up to their demands. Bill attributes his success to freshness. Everything, including the home fries and the egg salad, is made to order, nothing in advance. It takes more time but is worth the wait. His omelets are the most popular item. You design them with your choice of ten ingredients. The mushrooms are fresh, the cheese is real, the ham never boiled or canned. He cooks the eggs slowly on a huge flat grill, then rolls the extras up inside.

Bill goes to the loading docks each day to select his produce and other foods. He buys nitrate-free meat from a Dubuque, Iowa, butcher. And, he makes all his soups and desserts from scratch. He now uses more than 300 dozen eggs each week, and 400 pounds of potatoes.

His concept of freshness is carried through to the orange juice and coffee as well. When was the last time you were served a glass of fresh-squeezed orange juice in a restaurant? Bill grinds his own coffee beans, too. What a difference. And it may the first time you're ever served a cup of decaffeinated coffee that was brewed, not instant.

When you go to the Old Towne Cafe for your first visit, be prepared to wait. If you wonder what is taking so long, all you have to do is turn around and watch Bill at work.

"I could have made it myself by now," you might say. But, that's the point, Bill makes it just as you would at home. To do it right you have to do it yourself... or go to Old Towne Cafe.

How to get there: Take U.S. Hwy. 41 (which is the same as Tamiami Trail and 9th Street) to 285 9th Street.

While you're here: Naples' proximity to the Everglades allows visitors to experience some unusual scenery. Locals say the Corkscrew Swamp is your best bet. You can arrange for a guided tour at Wooten's via an air boat, an unusual pontooned water/swamp vehicle propelled by a giant fan. Locals also say the best time of year to visit Naples is in October, for Swamp Buggy Days. Named after another unusual vehicle that is a cross between an air boat and a four-wheel drive that was originally designed for hunting in marshy terrain, the festival includes a parade, the famous Swamp Buggy races and several other activities.

For those of you who enjoy window shopping, Naples "Old Town" offers close to the best in the state. The mile-square area is filled with gorgeous theme shops. Spend the day shopping and wind up with a sunset viewed from Naples Pier, just a few blocks west of Old Town.

CREAM OF MUSHROOM SOUP

3   **T. butter**
1   **lb. large, fresh mushrooms (sliced)**
1   **t. fresh garlic (minced, in jar)**
2   **c. beef stock (best if homemade but may substitute canned bouillon or consomme)**
2   **c. milk**
¼   **c. butter (melted)**
½   **c. flour**

1. Saute butter, mushrooms and garlic in large flat pan for several minutes.
2. Add beef stock. Boil mushrooms until dark brown (about 30 minutes).
3. Place mushroom mixture in double boiler. Add milk. Combine butter and flour in custard cup. Stir into a paste and then add a small amount of this mixture — a little at a time — to the double boiler. Stir well.
4. Simmer until thick (about 30 minutes). Stir often.

Serves: 4-6
Preparation: 10 minutes
Cooking: 1 hour

"Almost thick and rich enough to slice!"

— NOTES —

HOME FRIES

4   white idaho potatoes (washed)
1¾ c. chicken broth
8   slices bacon (each piece quartered)
2   medium onions (cut in 1" chunks)
1   t. paprika

1. Cook potatoes (with skins on) in chicken broth until done. Place in refrigerator and cool for several hours.
2. Cut chilled potatoes in 1¼" chunks.
3. Cook bacon until partially done. Then add onions and potatoes and brown nicely. Add paprika.

Serves: 4
Preparation: 15 minutes
Cooking: 20/10 minutes
Chill: 2 hours

*"I never knew potatoes could taste this fabulous...
make plenty!"*

— NOTES —

GENTLEMAN'S TOAST
(Herron Toast)

2	slices buffet ham
2	slices vienna or french bread
1-2	slices tomato
	garlic salt
	oregano
1	slice Swiss cheese
1	egg (beaten)

1. Saute ham slices, briefly. Place on 1 slice of bread.
2. Place tomato on ham. Sprinkle garlic and oregano over. Top with Swiss cheese and other slice of bread.
3. Dip the whole sandwich in egg and water.
4. Fry in pan on both sides until golden.

Serves: 1
Preparation: 5 minutes
Cooking: 5 minutes

"A nice hot sandwich for lunch — serve with gelatin salad!"

— NOTES —

Timmy's Nook

You won't know why, and you can't say now
Such a change upon you came,
But once you have slept on an island
You'll never be quite the same!
— Rachel Field, 1926

— Captiva Island —

Just as easily as an island's serene beauty contains the power
to change you, you have the power to change it. This recipro-
cal cause-effect relationship is exactly the Catch 22 syndrome
occurring on the west coast's Sanibel and Captiva Islands.
The name Sanibel is derived from the Spanish world *Sano*,
meaning healthy and *Bella*, meaning beautiful. Captiva is
named for the women that Jose Gaspar, a Spanish pirate is
said to have held captive there.

One woman whose roots are deeper into the islands' soil
than the Australian Pines that cover them is Charlotta Car-
per, co-owner of Timmy's Nook, one of Captiva Island's original structures. Charlotta is the third generation in her family
to live on the island. In the 1800s her grandmother traveled
from Canada and settled on nearby Buck Key. In 1925, the

family moved over to Sanibel Island. Here her parents bore seven daughters. In the 1950s, her father, Thomas Mahlon, built the restaurant, which, according to Charlotta, was primarily intended to be a means of escape from the female dominion of his household. The name Timmy's Nook was derived from her father's initials, T.M., which also became his nickname. T.M. eventually became Timmy.

Charlotta remembers when Captiva Island belonged only to those who had stewardship of the island, when the surrounding waters were so plentiful that they never bothered with the stone crabs. She remembers scallops as abundant as catfish in Lake Okeechobee. A favorite childhood game of the island — at one time encumbered with the fame of having the highest mosquito count in the world — was to place their hands against the screen door and wait for the mosquitoes to attack. When they took their hands away, distinct imprints remained where the mosquitoes were trying to bite through the screen.

Charlotta asserts all her efforts on behalf of the island's preservation. The Nook is, as it was, rustic, natural and homey.

When Islanders tell you to go eat crow, they are sending you to Timmy's Nook for a C.R.O.W. sandwich, but not derived from the winged version. The initials stand for Care and Rehabilitation of Wildlife, a local non-profit organization whose membership is dedicated to preserving the island wildlife, primarily birds. Many of the volunteers eat at Timmy's Nook and often order a sandwich they invented — a fish fillet, Swiss cheese, lettuce, tomato and onion on grilled rye bread, prepared much like a patty melt. The sandwich was named after the organization and is now a popular menu item.

The lunch menu features a variety of sandwiches, shrimp and clam baskets (always fresh), local stone crab claws (during season only), and homemade pies, all served in a naturally inviting, porch-like atmosphere overlooking Pine Island Sound.

The dinner menu, served after 5 p.m., is completely different. The chef and management put their hearts into the kitchen to cook up some incredible gourmet dishes.

Start your dinner with a steamed shrimp appetizer. They are perfectly prepared in boiling water and pickling spice. The difference is in the cooking time, David explains, just three minutes — no more — and don't wait for them to turn pink and float to the top.

Then try a cup of soup. The Nook's own New England Clam Chowder, made from scratch, is excellent. Or the Corn Chowder, which starts with a triple chicken stock every bit as good as Grandmother's.

On to an entree. Choices include a seafood platter, Shrimp Scampi (sauteed in butter, garlic, oregano and white wine on rice pilaf), Stone Crab Claws, Fried Clam Strips, Broiled Scallops (in butter and sherry), Surf 'n' Turf, and Crab Meat Crepes. The fish of the day is the most popular choice. Grouper, pompano, snapper, haddock, mackerel, tyle or flounder are the usual catches. You can have it broiled in lemon butter or lightly battered and fried. Occasionally barracuda is the featured catch. David says it is excellent and, prepared properly, perfectly safe. He adds that while many people avoid it because of the poisonous iodine sack just behind the head, he cuts it a good foot back from the mouth to avoid any danger of contaminating the fillets.

You may also sample the Crab Meat Crepes with Lemon-Cheese Sauce, and top your meal off with Charlotta's own famous Sour Cream Blueberry Pie. It is so popular that, for a recent festival featuring foods of the islands, she contributed 30 of her pies. In just 15 minutes, a dozen had been carted off by Islanders awaiting her arrival.

Captiva Island remains one of the most beautiful areas in the state, one that everyone should experience. But its beauty must not be harnessed in such a way that it becomes tarnished. If allowed to run free, nature will reproduce enough to be shared, preserving the natural health of the islands.

Come and enjoy your visit and respect the environment while you are here.

How to get there: Timmy's Nook is located at the big bend in Captiva Road at the near tip of the island. It may be reached via S.R. 867 off Hwy. 41 or Interstate 75 in Fort Myers. You can also come by boat via the Intracoastal Waterway. Closed Wednesdays.

While you're here: Residents say the best time of the year to visit the Islands is between May and November. They also recommend trying to make their annual festival the last weekend in April. There is always plenty to do on Captiva and Sanibel Islands. The beaches are unsurpassed anywhere in the state. You can rent a touring bicycle at several spots for a far better mode of transportation during the tourist season than your car. A popular and quite extraordinary resort is the South Seas Plantation, probably the best way to get a taste of island living.

QUICK CORN CHOWDER

2   c. whole kernel corn
3   slices bacon (cooked crisp and crumbled)
1   T. bacon drippings
1   c. cooked potatoes (diced)
¼   c. onion (minced)
1½ cans Legout mushroom soup (may substitute
    Campbell's Golden Mushroom Soup)
2   T. chopped pimiento
1½-2 c. real thick chicken broth
    (suggestion: 12 oz. jar Heinz Home Chicken Gravy)
½   c. butter
    beau monde seasoning to taste
    white pepper to taste
    dash marjoram

1. Combine all ingredients in large saucepan.
2. Heat to boiling and then simmer for 15 minutes.
3. Serve hot.

Serves: 4
Preparation: 20 minutes
Cooking: 20 minutes

"So rich, so thick, soooo...GOOD!"

— NOTES —

CRAB MEAT STUFFING

¾	c. water
½	c. butter
¼	c. white wine (chablis)
2	T. cooking sherry
½	t. white pepper
1½	t. salt
1	large onion (diced)
1	large green pepper (diced)
½	stalk celery (diced)
3	oz. milk (or half-n-half)
½	lb. snow crab crab meat
3	T. cornstarch
1	T. water
1	c. bread crumbs

1. Place first six ingredients in pot. Bring to boil. Add onion, green pepper and celery.
2. Return to boil and cook al dente. Add milk and crab meat.
3. Combine cornstarch and water in custard cup. Add to pot and cook until the consistency of wallpaper paste.
4. Reduce heat. Simmer for 5 minutes. Remove from heat. Add bread crumbs and stir well.
5. Fill split jumbo shrimp, flounder fillets, or crepes with stuffing.

Yield: 4 cups
Preparation: 20 minutes
Cooking: 15/10/5 minutes

"Adds a new dimension to fish, shrimp or crepes and easy to prepare."

CRAB MEAT CREPES WITH LEMON CHEESE SAUCE

— CREPE BATTER —

2	eggs
⅛	t. salt
1	c. flour
1	c. milk
¼	c. melted butter
	oil for frying

— LEMON CHEESE SAUCE —

¾	c. water
1	c. butter
1	t. salt
¼	t. white pepper
4	slices process Swiss cheese, cut in squares
2	T. cornstarch
1	T. water
2	T. lemon juice
¼	c. half-n-half

— CRAB MEAT STUFFING —
(See recipe on page 77)

— CREPES —

1. Combine eggs, salt, flour, milk and melted butter in mixing bowl. Beat for several minutes (or in blender for 1 minute).
2. Refrigerate for at least 1 hour before making up crepes.
3. Place a small amount of oil in bottom of 7½" or 9" fry pan. Add 2-3 T. batter and cook until done and lightly browned on one side.
   NOTE: Crepes can be made ahead and stored in refrigerator or freezer with layer of waxed paper between each crepe. Warm crepes before serving.

— LEMON CHEESE SAUCE —

4. Boil water, butter, salt and white pepper in pan.
5. Add Swiss cheese and stir until melted.

6.   Place cornstarch and water into custard cup, blend together and add to sauce in pot.
7.   Stir to thicken several minutes. Add lemon juice and half-n-half.
8.   Take 1 crepe and place on plate with non-browned side up. Add 1 large spoonful of crab meat stuffing along center of crepe. Fold ends over the filling.
9.   Top crepes with hot cheese sauce and serve.

Serves: 6
Preparation: 30 minutes
Cooking: 10 minutes (sauce)
          20 minutes (crepes)

"Much of this can be prepared ahead of time — great for a dinner party!"

— NOTES —

BLUEBERRY SOUR CREAM PIE

1   c. sugar
½   t. salt
¼   c. flour
2   eggs
2   c. sour cream
¾   t. almond extract
1   unbaked 9″ graham cracker pie shell
1   can blueberry pie filling

1.   In mixing bowl combine all ingredients except pie shell and pie filling. Mix well.
2.   Pour into pie shell and bake in 350°F. oven for 30 minutes or until center is set.
3.   Top hot pie with blueberries. Chill several hours.
4.   When ready to serve, top with Cool Whip or whipped cream.

Serves: 8
Preparation: 5 minutes
Cooking: 30 minutes
Chill: 2-3 hours

"Elegant looking...but easy!"

— NOTES —

— NOTES —

The Snook Inn, Matlacha, Florida

R. Stockey

Snook Inn

— Matlacha —

Where is Matlacha? Or, what is Matlacha? That's a typical reaction if you announce travel plans there. Matlacha (pronounced Mat-la-shay) is an obscure fishing village about 12 miles west of Fort Myers on the south end of Charlotte Harbor. It is a transitional community separating the bustling city of Fort Myers from rustic, undeveloped Pine Island. Just 20 miles separate the neighboring regions that are a world apart.

Matlacha is an island community where time has stood still. Like many of the Florida Keys, the village has grown to its natural limits. The original pathlike road built in 1926, connecting the network of islands, is now S.R. 78 connecting into the new Interstate 75 just east of Fort Myers. In 1968 the wooden bridge constructed over Matlacha Pass was replaced by a modern concrete lift span that is now known as Florida's most fished bridge.

At the foot of the west side of the bridge, you'll find the Snook Inn. This rustic and unintimidating restaurant was one of the first commercial establishments on the island, opening as a tavern in the 1940s.

Current owner Armand Marcotte, like many other residents of the area, landed here by accident on the recommendation of a man he met in the Carolinas on the way down from Illinois. Armand's career in his home state was in grocery management. He had passed the Snook Inn dozens of times before but never stopped in. That's quite understandable, as it isn't the type of place with a noticeably beckoning exterior, a category befitting many of the restaurants in this book.

But once you're inside, the charm of this seaside eatery is captivating. And the food is a perfect example of how it is possible for thousands of Floridians to live off the Gulf alone and enjoy variety as well. The menu is typical of hundreds of seafood shacks that are to be found in every beach community in Florida.

The menu is heavy on the "deep-fry," though the preparation method cuts down on the grease absorption. Deep-fried shrimp, oysters, grouper, scallops, flounder and crab cakes are served alone or in combination. You can also choose steamed shrimp, raw oysters or char-broiled grouper to get away from the fryer. An assortment of sandwiches, including hamburgers, ham n' cheese, BLT, chicken and roast beef are also available. If you're into oysters, try the oyster sandwich — regulars go nuts over it.

The lunch and dinner menus are nearly identical, with the exception of price, which jumps a couple of dollars.

Don't miss the Friday Night All-You-Can-Eat affair. Aside from the incredible value (all the grouper you can eat plus extras for only a few dollars), the place comes alive in local color. People from all over the Fort Myers area make the drive for this event. More than 200 pounds of grouper are dished out between late afternoon and early evening.

The ideal location of the Inn enhances the food's quality. Isn't it true that half of a dish's flavor is its visual effect? The Inn is located by the water, so close in fact, it is nearly *in* the water. If you sit in the center of the restaurant, you'll think you are on a houseboat. However, if you visit during the summer months, you would be wise to get there early to be assured of a seat on the screened porch as there is only a pleasant sea breeze for air conditioning. Armand says it doesn't bother people much as "they are willing to sweat it out for the Friday Night special."

The view is terrific from every seat in the house. To the east and south you look out on open water and uninhabited islands. The Matlacha Bridge provides interesting people-watching, especially after sundown when it comes alive with hopeful anglers. Many of them come into the Snook Inn to share fish tales over a shell of beer, which you can also order by the mug or the pitcher.

The Snook Inn is all that you would expect of a restaurant in a small fishing village as yet unspoiled by progress, an isolated seafood shack where you can enjoy Florida's fruits of the sea.

How to get there: From I-75 take S.R. 78 over the Matlacha Bridge. The Snook Inn is at the foot of the bridge on the left. You may also come by boat.

While you're here: If you're at all into fishing, this is said to be one of the best areas in the state for Snook, Redfish, Tarpon and Sheepshead. Grouper is also abundant. You can rent fishing boats or bring your own. You might also want to take one of the many "sunset cruises" available from the island.

A county park in Matlacha is the site for dozens of art fairs throughout the year, as well as an all-out Fourth of July celebration. Little Pine Island is a state preserve with a wide variety of natural wildlife and sea birds.

OYSTER SANDWICH

1 **large, whole oyster (fresh or canned)**
  1 can beer (domestic will do fine)
2 **T. buttermilk pancake mix**
  peanut oil (for frying)
  large bakery bun, grilled
  Swiss cheese slice
  tartar or cocktail sauce (best to use a *great* tartar sauce) (See recipe on page 87)

1. Take 1 oyster, dipping first in beer then in pancake mix. Deep fat fry in peanut oil which has been heated to 375°F.
2. Fry until oyster floats. Place on bun.
3. Place slice of Swiss cheese over top of oyster allowing heat from oyster to melt it.
4. Serve with tartar or cocktail sauce as preferred.

Serves: 1 sandwich per person
Preparation: 10 minutes
Cooking: 3-5 minutes per sandwich

"Oyster Heaven"

— NOTES —

TARTAR SAUCE

1   c. salad dressing
¼   c. dill relish
½   T. brown mustard (French's Bold & Spicy)

1. Combine the salad dressing, dill relish, and brown mustard. Mix well.
2. Refrigerate until needed.

Yield: 1 cup

"Simply Delicious"

— NOTES —

FRIED GROUPER

1   lb. grouper fillets (prefer fresh)
1   small can beer
1   c. buttermilk pancake mix (not the complete mix
    variety)
    peanut oil (for frying)

1. Cut fillets into fingers (about 1″ wide and 5″ long.)
2. Dip fingers into beer. Roll in pancake mix.
3. Heat peanut oil to 375 °F in deep fat fryer or pan
    with wire basket.
4. Drop freshly coated fingers into heated peanut oil.
    Cook for 3-4 minutes, until they float to the top and
    the outside darkens.
5. Serve with Snook Inn Tartar Sauce.
    (Recipe on page 87.)

Serves: 2
Preparation: 10 minutes
Cooking: 10 minutes

*"Despite its simplicity, everyone will ask how you make
this dish!"*

— NOTES —

SNOOK INN CRAB CAKES

2   c. water
2   c. instant mashed potatoes
2   T. butter
1   lb. crab meat (fresh or canned)
¼   c. minced onion
1   T. plus 1 t. mayonnaise
1¼   t. salt
1¼   t. Old Bay seasoning
1   T. Worcestershire sauce
1   T. baking powder
1   whole egg plus 1 egg white
     peanut oil (for frying)
     Snook Inn tartar sauce (See recipe on page 87)

1.   Heat water to boiling. Add potatoes and butter. Mix well and let cool in refrigerator until crab is fixed.
2.   Thoroughly rinse and drain crab meat. Using fingers, check through meat and remove any remaining pieces of shell or cartilage.
3.   Combine cooled potatoes, crab meat, and onion. Mix until well blended.
4.   Add remaining ingredients (except peanut oil). Mix well. Return to refrigerator. Chill for 3-4 hours.
5.   Heat peanut oil to 375°F. Make crab mixture into patties slightly smaller than desired cooked patty (they puff!)
6.   Cook patties until golden brown on both sides. They float on top. Serve with a good tartar sauce. (See recipe on page 87)

Serves: 6
Preparation: 30 minutes
Chill: 3-4 hours
Cooking: 10 minutes

"For an interesting luncheon dish serve on grilled bakery buns."

— NOTES —

State Farmers Market Restaurant

— Fort Myers —

When you see a convoy taking the Fort Myers Avenue exit off Interstate 75, there's a good chance the drivers are taking an "86" at the State Farmers Market Restaurant. The restaurant ranks high with produce truckers throughout Central Florida. And, though truckers aren't always known as purveyors of social graces, they are gourmets *par excellence* in discovering the best eating establishments.

The State Farmers Market Restaurant, so named for its location adjacent to the State Farmers Market, where produce is weighed, inspected and shipped to retail establishments, draws a large percentage of its clientele from this industry. But at all hours of the day, you'll also find a good number of area business employees, and, on Sundays, a majority of families enjoying home-style country cooking.

The restaurant has been the center landmark of the surrounding trucking companies for at least 25 years. Owners Karan Roach and her brother Bill Barnwell, born and raised in the area, purchased the 118-seat establishment in 1980, when the former owners retired. Recipes, menu and chefs remained the same.

For starters, every table is given a big basket of homemade cornbread to prepare your tummy for good things to come. More of it is smuggled out than is consumed on the premises, a much approved house custom. Karan says nearly 2,000 corn muffins are served each day over the weekend.

The decor, like the food, is plain and simple but warm and fulfilling. With cafe-style tables and chairs, booths along the windows and customers "howdy-ing" one another across tables, you might feel like you're an extra in a "Mel's Diner" episode, but everyone obviously loves the food here.

Live a little and try the deep-fried chicken gizzards and livers, unexpectedly delicious. The beef stew is also a treat — yes, folks, you can still find a hearty plate of homemade stew in a restaurant. And the grouper fingers and mullet draw raves, too.

All main dishes come with a choice of two farm-fresh vegetables that vary from day to day, and from season to season, including turnip greens, old-fashioned mashed potatoes with real gravy, blackeyed peas, candied yams, squash casserole and others.

The menu always includes a hand-written insert of daily specials, with special prices. According to Karan, many of the regulars are classified by the day of the week according to their favorite main courses.

Sundays are specially designed for families with old-fashioned feasts. The cooks are in the kitchen before dawn preparing things like Roast Duck with Brown Rice and Orange Sauce, Roast Leg of Lamb with Mint Jelly, Roast Turkey with Cornbread Dressing and Smoked Ham with Raisin Sauce. Three vegetables accompany these country-style meals, along with the cook's famous banana pudding. This is a great place to go for a nostalgic tour of how things used to be. Share it with your kids. If you do make it on a Sunday, expect a worthwhile wait. Families start lining up when church services are over. Sometimes, with customer approval, parties share tables. Karan is careful to matchmake wisely.

Saturdays are known for the Farmers Market's Okeechobee Catfish Special. Although in some parts of the country you're raised to get rid of a catfish as quickly as it grabs your line, including cutting the line if necessary, they are actually a delicious fresh-water fish and very popular in this state.

The State Farmers Market Restaurant is a choice vestige of country-style cooking and plenty of friendly local color in an urban community.

How to get there: 2736 Edison Avenue, Fort Myers. From Hwy. 41, go east on Anderson Avenue to Fowler Street. Take a right to Edison Avenue, then left to the Farmers Market on the south side of the road. You can also take Interstate 75 to the Anderson Avenue exit.

While you're here: You can walk some of your big meal off at the Coggins Trucking Company. The yard is filled with the finest trucking rigs found anywhere.

The Fort Myers Historical Museum, at 2300 Peck Street, is a recently completed restoration of the old Fort Myers railway depot. Though railroad exhibits are included, the focus of the museum is Southwest Florida regional history. It is open Tuesday through Friday.

STATE FARMERS MARKET RESTAURANT
FT. MYERS

DEEP FRIED CHICKEN LIVERS

1	lb. chicken livers*
1	c. milk
3	raw eggs
1	T. salt
1	T. black pepper
1	T. Vegit® (may substitute Spike seasoning)— Both can be found in any health food store)
½-1	c. flour
	oil for frying

1. Cut apart chicken livers if joined by membrane (you want individual livers).
2. Combine milk, eggs, salt, pepper, and Vegit® in bowl. Blend mixture with wire wisp.
3. Dip livers in egg batter and then into small amount of flour.
4. Heat oil in deep fat fryer to 375°F. Cook livers 'til golden brown (about 5 minutes). Serve hot.

Serves: 6 as a main dish or 20-25 appetizers
Preparation: 5 minutes
Cooking: 15 minutes

"These are delicious — even for non-liver lovers!"

*NOTE: Substitute gizzards for livers if you desire or use a combination of the two.

— NOTES —

CHICKEN WITH YELLOW RICE PILAF

1	3 lb. fryer chicken, cut up
2	c. cold water
1	T. yellow food coloring
½	c. celery (diced)
½	c. cup green pepper (diced)
½	c. onion (diced)
1	t. Accent
½	t. black pepper
2	chicken bouillon cubes
1	c. long grain raw rice

1. Place chicken, water, and food coloring in large saucepan. Stir.
2. Add the remaining ingredients except rice. Stir to mix well.
3. Cover and cook for 45 minutes to 1 hour or until chicken is almost done.
4. Add rice. Cover and cook until rice is partially cooked. Remove lid and finish cooking until rice is cooked and dry.
5. Serve. Excellent with tossed salad or fruited gelatin salad.

Serves: 3-4
Preparation: 10 minutes
Cooking: 1½ hours

"An easy dish to prepare with a great blending of flavors!"

— NOTES —

STATE FARMERS MARKET RESTAURANT
FT. MYERS

TURNIP GREENS WITH ROOTS

1   box turnip greens with chopped pieces (frozen)
½   c. salt pork (diced)
1½   c. cold water
½   c. margarine
      salt and pepper to taste

1. Place greens in shallow 2-quart pot. Add salt pork and water.
2. Bring to boil. Simmer for 1 hour.
3. Add margarine. Cook for 15 minutes.
4. Salt and pepper to taste.

Serves: 3-4
Preparation: 5 minutes
Cooking: 1 hour

"A good southern favorite that is easy to prepare!"

— NOTES —

SPICED APPLES

1	16 or 20 oz. can sliced apples
¾	c. granulated sugar
1	t. nutmeg
1	t. cinnamon
1	t. allspice
1	T. imitation vanilla flavoring (can also use vanilla extract)
1	c. cold water

1. Drain apples and place in shallow baking pan.
2. Combine all other ingredients. Mix well with apples.
3. Cover pan with aluminum foil and bake in 375°F oven for 45 minutes.
4. Serve hot.

Serving Suggestions: Serve over Vanilla Pudding, Tapioca or Ice Cream!

Serves: 4
Preparation: 5 minutes
Cooking: 45 minutes

"Easy . . . could be the spice of life!"

— NOTES —

Flora & Ella's Restaurant, LaBelle, Florida

Flora and Ella's Restaurant

From Northern California to Southern Alabam,
And little towns across the land,
We can skin bucks and run a trout line.
Country folks can survive.

We grow our own tomatoes,
Make our own wine too,
Ain't too many things we can't do.
Country folks can survive.

— LaBelle —

Flora and Ella's Restaurant in LaBelle, between Fort Myers and Lake Okeechobee, is a story of survival, both for its owners and for the restaurant itself. Flora Hampton and Ella Burchard are the sisters who own the restaurant, though recently Flora left the business to care for their mother, Corine Forrey, a lifetime resident and pioneer of LaBelle.

Flora, Ella, their sister Ida and Mrs. Forrey are all part of the Burke family, who have been a part of this "City in the Oaks" since before the turn of the century. Before them, the area belonged only to the Caloosa Indians who traveled from all parts of Florida to the banks of the nearby Caloosahatchee River to hold religious ceremonies. They were later driven away by the Seminole Indians and the "white man," who fought each other for rights to the area. Outposts were built to protect settlers during the Seminole Wars. Most have disappeared.

The year 1880 marked 50 years of boom-time growth for La-Belle. Steamboat traffic on the Caloosahatchee brought hundreds of pioneers to the community, which marked the end of the navigable water until a canal was dredged to Lake Okeechobee in the early '30s as part of Herbert Hoover's plan for depression recovery.

It was this canal project that brought Flora and Ella's restaurant into its heyday.

Ella's grandmother lived here in the 1800s. She was the only "doctor" in the area, making medicines from herbs found in the woods. Ella says that women in her day "didn't make a big deal out of getting their equal opportunity rights...they just took them."

Ella's mother was born near LaBelle. After marrying, she and her husband opened a grocery store and meat market. Most of the other early settlers made their living from orange groves and cattle.

Then came Ella, Flora and Ida. The family survived two hurricanes, one in '26 and another in '28, that completely washed away several surrounding communities. Ella remembers a 20-foot wave surge off Lake Okeechobee.

They also survived an era of gangsters. "The Ashley Gang" caused a wave of crime and violence in the area. Her father, a captain of one of the dredging boats, uncovered the body of one of their many victims.

Ella married. When the depression came, the entire community became terribly distressed. Ella's husband survived by going out into the woods (what is now the Immokalee area, called the "last frontier") to cut trees for lumber. He cleared his own trails by hand, set up a rough sawmill, and hauled out the logs. Ella wouldn't hear from him for long periods of time, but they survived. Many didn't. In 1933, her husband built her a log cabin from which to operate a restaurant with her sisters. She had been running a small hamburger stand while he was gone. Everything in the cabin, including the stools and lamps, was hand-carved from pine.

In 1943, the restaurant was moved to the present location at the intersection of Bridge and Ft. Thompson on Hwy. 29. It was also the Post Office, the Bus Depot, and the Freight Station serving the area. Just about everyone in town had reason to go by Flora and Ella's each day. By this time, the river dredging had tripled the town population, and the restaurant was the only one in town.

Flora and Ella's is still recognized as the place to go for the best food in the area. Little has changed, inside or out. Though the Post Office is gone, Ella still sells bus tickets and operates the oldest Western Union office in the state. The tables and chairs are the same, as are the soda fountain and counter, and the sundries cases. Many younger people have little recollection of the days when going for a malt or soda meant a walk through the sundries department. Ella says she used to do a big business of it, but now sales representatives no longer call on her. Some of the products behind the antique glass cases look more valuable as collectibles than their original sales price.

You'll also see an old-time phone booth inside the restaurant. Ella says it was installed in the 1940s, and though the phone company wants to replace it, she won't let them.

The menu features home cooking created by Ella and Eula Mae, who has been with her for 20 years. It is almost exactly as it was in the '40s. Ella calls it soul food, though the term has only recently become popular. She says it is the food that pioneers were made of. Blackeyed peas with rice and fresh onion, fresh collard greens, swamp cabbage, catfish (She calls them "sharpies"), cornbread and hushpuppies, and chicken and dumplings are popular and delicious, as are her famous "mile-high" pies and cakes.

The soda fountain produces old-fashioned cones, malts, sodas and sundaes served to recall past memories, with no paper cups or plastic spoons. LaBelle kids don't know how good they have it.

Ella's husband still owns a sawmill in town, her sons are successful and living nearby. And, she can now boast of the fact that her family is in its seventh generation in LaBelle! Their roots are as far into the soil as the oaks the town is famous for. Their story of survival is as rich in excitement, strength, and love as *Little House on the Prairie*, Southern style.

How to get there: *On the intersection of Bridge and Ft. Thompson on Hwy. 29. Take Hwy. 80 east from Interstate 75, or west from the Florida Turnpike, to LaBelle. Turn North on 29 to the restaurant on west side of the road, 1½ blocks south of the bridge.*

While you're here: *Across from Flora and Ella's, you'll find an endangered species, a family-owned hardware business that hasn't "flowed with the times." Jennings Hardware was opened in LaBelle in 1911 by L.M. Jennings, the current owner's grandfather. It is a wonderful journey into the past . . . nails "by the pound" in steel bins, gadgets, the distinctive old-time hardware aroma, and the personal touch. Tom Woosley, owner, and all his sons now run the business. Take your kids for a history lesson.*

And, if you're lucky enough to come through town during the LaBelle Swamp Cabbage Festival, the third weekend in February, you are in for a special treat. The festival is dedicated to the Sabal Palm (or cabbage palm), Florida's state tree. It attains a height of 80 feet with a two-foot trunk diameter if not cut down for food or fiber first. The heart of the palm, a three-foot bud, is cut from the three- to five-year-old tree to produce one of the most delicious vegetables you'll ever taste, swamp cabbage. Ecologists take note: a cut tree reproduces several offspring by natural seeding. The fiber of these trees, harvested near LaBelle, is the only natural brush fiber grown and processed in the United States. The fiber, taken from young trees, is used all over the world in various brushes and brooms. The festival delivers a myriad of swamp cabbage recipes prepared as patties, fritters, salads, casseroles, and combined with game or salt pork. Three days of unusual events also accompany the feasts.

SWAMP CABBAGE SALAD

1   **head lettuce, torn into bite-size pieces**
1   **avocado**
2   **c. raw swamp cabbage* (soak in strong salt water 20 minutes and drain) (May substitute 2 large cans of Hearts of Palm, found in Gourmet Specialty Shops and Supermarkets.)**
    French dressing
    salt and lots of pepper to taste
    *Also known as Sabal Palm

1. Gently toss salad ingredients. Add French dressing. Toss again.
2. Salt and pepper to taste.

    *Note: At this time the Sabal Palm is not a state protected species. However, many counties in Florida regulate and protect the species. If you desire the raw cabbage, be sure to call your local county government and ask for local regulations regarding the palm.

Serves: 4-6
Preparation: 20 minutes soak/5 minutes

"A refreshing salad on a hot summer's day!"

— NOTES —

SWAMP CABBAGE WITH TOMATOES

½   c. salt pork or slab bacon (diced)
½   c. onions (diced)
1   14 oz. can swamp "cabbage" (Hearts of Palm)
1   16 oz. can sliced stewed tomatoes
    salt and pepper to taste

1.   Place salt pork or slab bacon in 2-quart saucepan and cook for a few minutes over low heat.
2.   Add onion to pan and saute until onion is slightly browned and transparent.
3.   Slice swamp cabbage across the stalks into ¼-½" slices. Add to saucepan.
4.   Add the remaining ingredients and mix well. Cook until cabbage is done, about 10-15 minutes.

Serves: 4
Preparation: 5 minutes
Cooking: 20-25 minutes

"A delicious vegetable to serve with fish, meat, or poultry."

— NOTES —

SWAMP CABBAGE PATTIES

2   c. cooked swamp cabbage* (drained — may substitute 2 cans Hearts of Palm, found in Gourmet Specialty Shops and Supermarkets)
1   c. water
½   c. onion (finely chopped)
1   egg (slightly beaten)
     salt and lots of pepper to taste
     flour
     bacon fat or cooking oil

1. Cook swamp cabbage partially in water. Be sure to cook with lots of pepper.
2. Remove from pot and dice. Combine with onion, egg, salt, and pepper. Add flour a little at a time until stiff.
3. Heat griddle or frying pan with 1″ fat in bottom. Drop mixture by teaspoon into hot grease. Fry until brown. Serve hot.

*Note: In the matter of black pepper in swamp cabbage we must refer to Mark Twain's statement pertaining to the amount of Bourbon to put in egg nog, "Too much is exactly enough." Regardless of the amount used, it is essential that the pepper be cooked with the cabbage.

Serves: 6
Preparation: 10 minutes
Cooking: 10 minutes

"You'll be swamped with extra dinner guests after this one!"

CHICKEN WITH DUMPLINGS

1   large chicken (about 3-3½ lbs.) (cleaned)
1-1½ qts. water
1   small onion (chopped)
2   stalks celery (chopped)
1   t. salt
1   t. black pepper
1   c. flour
      pinch baking powder
1   large egg
¼-⅓ c. chicken broth
      salt and pepper to taste

1. In large pot place chicken, water, onion, celery, salt, and pepper.
2. Cook chicken until done. Remove from broth and allow to cool.
3. In bowl place flour and baking powder. Make deep well in center. Add egg and chicken broth.
4. Gently beat egg and broth together. Mix in surrounding flour. Form into ball.
5. Pinch small amount of dough and roll on floured board. Roll **very thin**.
6. Cut into ½" strips and drop into boiling chicken broth. Cook slowly until tender.
7. Meanwhile, pick meat from chicken. Cut into bite-size pieces and return to pot with dumplings once they are tender.
8. Heat through and thicken with flour if necessary.

Serves: 6
Preparation: 20 minutes
Cooking: 40 minutes

"Good down-home stick-to-the-rib cookin'!"

CORNMEAL MUFFINS

1	c. flour
1	c. cornmeal
¼	c. sugar
¼	t. salt
4	t. baking powder
	pinch baking soda
2	large eggs
1	c. buttermilk
⅓	c. melted butter

1. Mix flour, cornmeal, sugar, salt, baking powder, and baking soda.
2. Add eggs, buttermilk, and butter. Blend until just moistened. (Do not overmix.)
3. Grease 18-cup muffin pans (or use non-stick pan). Fill cups three-quarters full.
4. Bake in 425°F oven about 10 minutes.

Yield: 18
Preparation: 10 minutes
Cooking: 10 minutes

"An old Southern favorite!"

— NOTES —

PEAS AND RICE

— RICE —

1   c. rice (long-grain white)
2   c. water
2   t. salt
2   T. butter

— PEAS —

2   c. water
1   lb. fresh blackeyed peas (may substitute frozen)
¼   lb. salt pork (diced)
1   small onion (finely chopped)

1. Wash rice in water. In heavy pot combine rice, water, salt and butter. Cover.
2. Bring to boil, then simmer until dry. Do not stir.

— PEAS —

3. Bring the water to a boil. Add peas and salt pork. Cook until tender (45 minutes-1 hour).
4. Serve rice in an attractive bowl. Top with peas and "pot liquor" (juice from bottom). Sprinkle chopped onions over all. Enjoy.

Serves: 4
Preparation: 5 minutes
Cooking: 20 minutes/1 hour

"With corn meal muffins and butter, what a meal!"

— NOTES —

FRESH COCONUT CAKE

1	box cake mix (white, yellow or chocolate)
16	oz. coconut (frozen or canned moist)
16	oz. sour cream
2	c. sugar
9	oz. whipped topping (Cool Whip)

1. Prepare cake mix according to directions baking in 3-9″ layers (it will take less time than directions say so watch carefully 10 minutes before end of baking time).
2. Combine coconut, sour cream and sugar. Let stand 2 hours.
3. After cake has cooled place one layer on serving plate.
4. Reserve one-half cup of coconut mixture for topping on bottom layer.
5. Place second layer on top and use remaining half of coconut mixture to cover. Follow with third layer.
6. Mix the one-half cup reserved coconut mixture together with whipped topping. Frost top and sides of cake with it.
7. Refrigerate for 2 days before serving.

Yield: 1-9″ cake
Preparation: 20 minutes
Cooking: 25 minutes
Chill: 2 days

"If you can manage to keep little fingers out of the cake until it's set — the wait is worth it!"

— NOTES —

Ye Tower Lunch

For as I like a young man in whom there is something of the old, So I like an old man in whom there is something of the young. And he who follows this maxim, in body will possibly be an old man, but he will never be an old man in spirit.
— Cicero

— Lantana —

Paul Dunbar, owner of Ye Tower Lunch in Lantana, is not only a seasoned cook, but also a living historical essay on this small beach community just outside of West Palm Beach.

He has been cooking for Lantanians for more than half a century. He is now in his eighties, witty, intelligent, and hardworking.

Paul moved to Boynton Beach, five miles south of Lantana, from New York in 1924 with his brother. They opened a restaurant there to accommodate the wave of prospective real estate buyers who were arriving by the busload, literally, from northern states. In 1925, they were asked to come up to Lantana to bid on "The Tower." The 55-foot tower had been constructed by a real estate developer, A.O. Greynolds, to be used as a look-out platform to show prospective property buyers the plats they might be interested in. According to Paul, you could see everything within 20 miles of the site from the top. Paul and his brother purchased the structure and made it the home of Ye Tower Lunch, to service the four-year-old community of just 100 residents.

The following year, Dixie Highway (Hwy. 1) was constructed just a few feet in front of the restaurant. Real estate was booming, and several developers were sending buses up to Northern cities to bring people down to look at property. Ye Tower was one of the rest stops, keeping Paul busy in the kitchen.

As the population of the area grew, Ye Tower became "the spot" for socializing. Paul says his place would be packed after community events and high school dances. Ye Tower was always included in date plans. Though the actual restaurant accommodated no more than 30 people, the 55-foot tower allowed plenty of room for intimacy. It seems not everyone came just to enjoy Paul's excellent home-cooked meals.

Ye Tower's tower crashed to its death in the hurricane of 1928. The entire town mourned the occasion. A miniature version, just five feet tall, was constructed atop the restaurant as a memorial to its service to the community.

Paul's brother moved on after the war, but Paul stayed with the restaurant. He opened a drive-in area and hired "curb boys." Women hadn't made it into this corner of the job market at that time.

Paul became as popular in town as his restaurant. In 1940, he was placed on the town council where he served as a councilman until he was elected mayor in 1948. He served as mayor for nine years until 1957 when he was replaced because many thought he was too old. That was more than two decades ago.

One of the projects Paul spear-headed as mayor, Lantanians may be especially grateful for. He had the city purchase a

110-foot by 3,000-foot strip of beach for $80,000 to belong exclusively and eternally to the public.

In between running the restaurant and the city, Paul also became one of the area's most respected photographers. Most of the photos in Lantana's archives of the earliest days of development are his work.

Today, he is content with letting his successors run the city while he runs the restaurant, though he is certainly not sitting back. He is open for breakfast, lunch and dinner six days a week, and always on the premises. He once lived in the restaurant, but now has a small home behind it.

The oldest continuous-ownership business in the county, the tiny restaurant looks much as it did in 1925. About the only change is the absence of French doors on either corner of the building. Twice the restaurant had cars drive right through the wall, resulting in some extensive reconstruction. Paul says he now worries more about cars blowing through than hurricanes. The restaurant is only a foot off the highway. A grandfather clause in the deed prevents the city from moving it back.

Inside are the original soda fountain, ice cream case, counter and stools, clocks and the original plate glass candy cases. Much of the tableware and soda glasses date back to the '20s as well. Paul even cooks from a Fanny Farmer Cookbook dated 1919. Good cooking may not age, but the book certainly has.

The soda fountain is alive and well at Ye Tower. Paul will make you an old-fashioned chocolate malt, served in an old-time malt glass and soda spoon, that will make you feel ten years old again.

You can fall head-over-heels for his corned beef hash, made from scratch. Though Paul says his food is very basic, his nearly 60 years of experience make the difference.

How to get there: 916 So. Dixie Hwy. Take the Florida Turnpike to the Osborne Road exit. Go east to Hwy. 1 (Dixie Highway) and south to the restaurant.

While you're here: Head back up the road five miles to West Palm Beach and try your luck at the dog tracks (January to May), at the Palm Beach Kennel Club, or Jai-Alai (November to March) at the West Palm Beach Fronton. Both are popular Floridian activities.

OLD FASHION MALTS

2   **ample scoops vanilla ice cream**
½   **c. milk**
1½ **T. malted milk**
1½ **oz. (scant ¼ c.) chocolate syrup**

1.   Combine all ingredients in blender. Mix for just 5 seconds.
2.   Pour into soda glass. Serve immediately. (If desired garnish with dolup of whipped cream and cherry)

Serves: 1
Preparation: 5 seconds

"For kids only, or adults young at heart."

— NOTES —

CORNED BEEF HASH

3   T. bacon fat (or use Crisco)
1   lb. can corned beef
3   potatoes (boiled, peeled, and sliced into flat
     walnut-size pieces)*
1   large onion (diced)
     salt & pepper
     Optional: 4 poached eggs

1.   Heat fat in skillet (A preseasoned cast iron skillet
     works best.)
2.   Add corned beef (broken into small pieces),
     potatoes, and onions.
3.   Season with salt and pepper. Fry until brown.
4.   Each serving may be served with optional poached
     egg placed on top.

     *Boil potatoes with skins on until done. Place in
     refrigerator and when ready to use, take out ahead
     of time. Inside moisture will cause skins to
     separate from potatoes and come out of jackets
     easily.

Serves: 4
Preparation: 15 minutes
Cooking: 15 minutes

"A quick and filling lunch dish for the hearty appetite!"

— NOTES —

Sage Bagel & Appetizer Shop

Sage Bagel and Appetizer Shop

— Hallandale —

The owners of Sage Bagel and Appetizer Shop, in Hallandale on the north side of Miami, set an excellent example of the traits that produce success.

Milton Fuerst and Sid Eichen brought their culinary expertise to Florida's Gold Coast in 1973. Milton had spent 25 years in the bagel business in the eastern section of New York City known as Queens. Ironically, the bricks used in his old-fashioned bagel oven were the reason for his city-wide fame. Yet it was bricks hurled through his window that influenced his decision to move away. When vandalism affected the neighborhood, Milton concluded it was a sign to move his bagel business to the "Promised Land." He and his wife, Iris, searched the state for a suitable and affordable location in vain. He had given up, deciding to try Arizona, when driving down barren Hallandale Boulevard on his way to the airport, a man was pounding in a "Store for Rent" sign. This was it.

When Sid Eichen, a successful owner of an appetizer shop in New York, heard of Milton's move, he was one of the few who believed a New York City bagel could be transplanted to

South Florida. He would join Milton . . . It would be a perfect partnership. Sid was born behind a counter, his parents having owned grocery stores with appetizer sections in both Poland and America. Milton's wife's family had always been bakers, and he was a bagel perfectionist. They would have to be made in a brick oven, a practice rarely adhered to in modern production methods. The 14-foot chamber was reconstructed — brick by brick by Old World craftsmen flown down from New York.

Today, it is obvious that the transplant was well accepted. After all, many of Miami's residents are New York transplants themselves. It isn't uncommon for Milton and Sid to see the familiar faces of loyal customers from their former shops. And many of the staff, including Stanley Drucker, who creates the salads and spreads, were former employees or kosher competitors.

The shop, which has already been expanded, includes Milton's "bagel factory," producing bagels totally unlike any you've ever tasted. Watching is half the fun. When the dough is just right, it is pulled off in strips and hand-rolled around his three middle fingers. Shaping, according to Milton, is the crucial stage. The hole must be the perfect size. Then the bagels are placed on wooden boards for the yeast to react to the malt and rise. Next they're dropped into a four-foot kettle of boiling water. Milton says the water takes away the starch from the dough, which is high in gluten and low in cholesterol. Then it's back to the boards where they are flavored with sesame, garlic, poppy seed or fresh onion. Finally, they go into the 550°F brick oven where they revolve for 15 minutes. It's the brick that gives the bagels flavor, a crispy exterior and soft inside. The creation of one of the world's most versatile and internationally popular foods is truly an art form.

Because thousands of these "holey" delicious treats are served each day, they are served hot from the oven. The only tough part of the bagel experience is deciding what to put on it. The display cases contain a variety of salads and spreads including liver pate, vegetable cream cheese, scallion cheese, chopped herring, chicken salad, baked salmon salad, and mushroom and egg salad, which is a Sage original. Whatever your choice, it is heaped on the toasted bagel for a tasty and filling quick lunch.

You can also top it with a kosher choice of nova and cream cheese. Sid's end of the shop offers the widest variety of smoked fish anywhere in Florida. The selection includes lox, salmon, white fish, sable, filet of herring in white sauce, gaspe nova, Michigan chubs and genuine Canadian lake sturgeon, a very expensive delicacy. The kosher deli department adds another list of choices with delicious cold cuts including pastrami, corned beef and salami. And finally, there are hundreds of international bulk cheeses to add to your bagel dressing.

When you've finally made your choice, you can add to your meal a salad from several gourmet concoctions; potato knishes, a fabulous mashed and spiced potato mixture in flaky pastry; chicken soup with matzoh balls; or one of dozens of other kosher treats. If you are new to Jewish foods, it will take you hours to review the entire inventory.

The Sage Bagel and Appetizer Shop has succeeded in putting Hallandale on the map — the world map. Special orders for their kosher specialties have been sent to Columbia, Brazil, Argentina, Toronto, Montreal, and even to the workers on the north slope of the Alaska pipeline. More than a thousand customers pour in each day.

The final irony, says Sid, is that vacationing New Yorkers are loading up with Florida bagels to take home with them.

Despite the international acclaim, Milton says he was truly confident of the delicatessen's success only when a recent customer told him that her cab driver, who hadn't said a word since they left the airport, pointed to the Sage Plaza and blurted, "There's the Sage Bagel Shop!"

How to get there: 800 East Hallandale Boulevard, Hallandale. Take Interstate 95, or the Florida Turnpike, to the Hallandale Boulevard exit (Hwy. 824). Turn east to the address. The shop is in the Sage Plaza on the south side of the road.

While you're here: The horse track is one of the most popular activities. It is located on U.S. 1 and Hallandale Boulevard, and open only in the spring. Just a few miles north, the Hollywood Boardwalk is a two-mile long, 24-foot wide oceanfront promenade that provides the area's best people-watching, as well as memorable natural scenery.

CHOPPED LIVER

1½ **lb. mild sweet onions, Bermuda or Spanish (chopped)**
½ **lb. chicken livers**
4 **hard boiled eggs**
1 **c. vegetable oil**
salt and pepper to taste

1. Saute liver and onions til brown, mixing thoroughly.
2. Combine liver, onions and eggs in food processor or blender.
3. Mix until mixture is of spreading consistency.
4. Add salt and white pepper to taste.
5. Serve on party rye, crackers, bagels, or stuff into celery or as an appetizer, garnished.

Makes: 3-4 cups
Preparation: 15-20 minutes
Chill: ½ hour

"A delicious blending of flavors — Make plenty — It will go fast!"

— NOTES —

VEGETABLE CREAM CHEESE

1   c. minced fresh vegetables (even amounts of green pepper, peeled cucumbers, radishes, scallions, shredded carrots)
2½   8 oz. pkg. cream cheese, softened

1. Mix vegetables and cream cheese together well.
2. Chill or serve immediately.

    *NOTE: Spread on snack breads, bagels, or crackers.

Makes: 3-4 cups
Preparation: 20 minutes
Chill: 1-2 hours

"Luscious especially when you have access to variety of fresh vegetables. Delicious to snack on and very nutritious too!"

— NOTES —

MUSHROOM AND EGG SALAD BAGEL SANDWICH

½   lbs. mushrooms (chopped)
2   lbs. onions (chopped)
10 boiled and peeled eggs
½   c. Matzo meal
1   c. vegetable oil
    salt and white pepper

1. Saute mushrooms and onions in vegetable oil until brown. BE CAREFUL NOT TO BURN.
2. Chop eggs and place in food processor.
3. Grind all ingredients together until chunky (not pureed).
4. Add Matzo meal, salt, and pepper.
5. Spread on bagel or crackers or serve as an appetizer, garnished.

Makes: 3-4 cups
Preparation: 15-20 minutes
Cooking: ½ hour

"A nutritious luncheon or snack dish!"

— NOTES —

Bimini Sea Shack

— Ft. Lauderdale —

Fort Lauderdale, along with being recognized as one of the fastest growing cities in the world, has been called the "Venice of America." The 170 miles of canals that form a unique waterway network of transportation are also the backdrop of most of the city's residential dwellings. The city, quite obviously, has more pleasure boats registered than any other city in Florida. Its nickname is also appropriate in describing the area's European flavor which is reflected in the sophistication of its cultural activities, the quality and diversity of its food and the number of guests the city hosts from other countries.

Choosing just one "underground" restaurant to represent a city that lists 32 pages of restaurants in its yellow pages is at best a painstaking task. But it helps to discover that a good percentage of the Bimini Sea Shack's customers who travel by boat from several Caribbean Islands and the Bahamas make this restaurant their first stop after docking, claiming to plan their food choices while crossing the Atlantic.

Owner Hazel Day draws from her own vast traveling experience, which centers around fishing, in areas such as Alaska, Aruba and the Bahamas. She creates her own recipes for the seafood dinners served here. A fisherman in her own right, she is thoroughly familiar with locating the best catches, which waters produce the best of each variety, and how to prepare them to enhance their flavor, rather than conceal it.

The small restaurant is divided by the kitchen into two parts. One side is a pub catering to young people. Hazel has a soft spot in her heart for youth, having raised seven children in Fort Lauderdale. The other side is the eating area, seating about 30 customers. An island aura is created by plants, a couple of fan-back wicker chairs, and ceiling fans.

When you arrive, daughter Bonnie brings the chalkboard menu to your table. The choices vary from day to day, but include Linguine with Clam Sauce, Broiled Grouper, Garlic Shrimp, Steamed Clams, Mussels, Broiled Bluefish, Snapper and Dolphin, Conch Chowder, Conch Fritters and Conch Salad.

All of the recipes are the result of years of experimentation. Son Allen, a boat captain, would bring her mussels, conch and assorted catches with which to experiment. She has developed a style that is all her own and compiled the recipes in a cookbook that is available in the restaurant.

Most of her dishes are very spicy. Bonnie warns diners of this and if they express any objection, she steers them to menu items that are less so. If Hazel were to put a label on her cooking, she would call it Bahamian.

Broiled Grouper — the house specialty — goes well with a side order of Conch Salad, preceded by a basket of Hazel's own Bimini Bread, straight from the oven. Hazel's secret is the use of powdered milk, an ingredient necessary to substitute in the Bahamas, where fresh milk is a precious commodity.

Servings of grouper fillet are enormous, at least 1½" thick and extending beyond the edges of the plate. It comes smothered in onions and basted with a garlic marinade. The dinner is accompanied by a large serving of Hazel's hash browns, coated with herbs and spices, more like the texture and appearance of scalloped potatoes than that of fried potatoes.

You might also want to sample the "steamers " (steamed clams) — the portions are incredible! And, Hazel does the clamming herself. King Crab is also a specialty, and there are other choices if you prefer something besides seafood.

Hazel and Bonnie relate best to boat people, as every member of the family is, or was, a sailor. Several pictures of their boats and boating excursions are on the wall. Hazel is as well versed in fish tales as she is in sailing stories, keeping her customers well entertained.

How to get there: *1465 State Road 84, Fort Lauderdale. Take Interstate 95 or the Florida Turnpike to the S.R. 84 exit in Fort Lauderdale. Head east to the address, on the north side of the road. Open evenings Monday through Saturday.*

While you're here: *Fort Lauderdale is one of the most culturally active areas in the state, with several museums and small theater groups. You may enjoy the Museum of the Arts on Las Olas Boulevard, or the Parker Playhouse on N.E. 8th Street. Your family will find Ocean World an educational experience. For gamblers, there are the Dog Races in Hollywood, Jai-Alai in Dania, Harness Racing in Pompano Park and the Horse Track in Hallandale. And for naturalists, the Hugh Taylor Birch State Recreation Area on A1A and Sunrise Blvd. is a 180-acre rustic park in the heart of the city, right across the street from the ocean. Two fresh-water lagoons, nature trails, fishing, boating and miniature passenger trains touring the park are there for family fun.*

BIMINI BREAD

3   **cakes yeast**
¾   **c. powdered dry milk**
1   **c. sugar**
¾   **c. oil**
½   **t. salt**
3   **eggs**
2½   **c. warm water**
5   **pounds all-purpose flour (sifted)**

1. Using food processor, mixer, or hand, beat together yeast, dry milk, sugar, oil, salt, eggs, and ½ c. warm water.
2. In large pan pour the above ingredients. Add 2 c. warm water and slowly add the flour, several cups at a time, stirring well after each addition.
3. Knead in bowl. Let rise until double.
4. Place on large floured board. Knead until all air is out.
5. Cut into 7 pieces.
6. Place in buttered loaf pans or large cake pans.
7. Let loaves rise until double. Bake 30 minutes in 350°F oven.
8. Freeze extra loaves when cooled for future use.

Makes: 7 loaves
Preparation: 3-4 hours
Cooking: 30 minutes

"We have not reduced this recipe from the original. By using this exact recipe — unaltered — you will achieve the perfect results as experienced at the Bimini. Make this full recipe and always have homemade bread on hand!"

— NOTES —

BANANA DUFF

½   c. butter
½   c. sugar
2   eggs
2   c. flour
1   t. baking powder
¾   c. milk
    bananas (cut in 1-2" pieces)
    flour
    water

1. Cream butter and sugar together. Add eggs and beat thoroughly.
2. Sift flour and baking powder together. Add alternately to creamed mixture along with milk. Form into ball.
3. Place flour on counter or board. Roll out dough as you would a pie crust. Cut into sections and roll around banana pieces.
4. Cook in water on top of double boiler until dough is done.

Makes: 1-2 dozen
Preparation: 10 minutes
Cooking: 10-15 minutes

"Serve as a side dish with entree or sprinkle with cinnamon-sugar mixture!"

— NOTES —

BIMINI SEA SHACK
FT. LAUDERDALE

BIMINI KEY LIME PIE

1 can sweetened condensed milk
1 8 oz. pkg. cream cheese, softened
½-¾ c. juice from Key Limes (other limes will do, but not as tasty)
½ t. vanilla
1 9″ graham cracker pie crust
Whipped cream topping

1. Combine milk, cream cheese, and lime juice in blender. Blend on low speed until smooth.
2. Add vanilla and stir into mixture.
3. Pour into graham cracker crust.
4. Chill in refrigerator until set.
5. Top with whipped cream before serving.

Serves: 8
Preparation: 5 minutes
Chill: 3-4 hours

"Perfect blending of flavors and so easy!"

— NOTES —

— NOTES —

Lime Tree Bay Café, Long Key, Florida

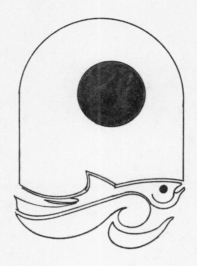

The Lime Tree Bay Cafe

— Long Key —

It is amazing how many Floridians have never been to the Florida Keys. There is a rich tapestry of travel experiences in the state's own backyard. No matter how many times you visit, you will always be thrilled by a new experience.

Even if you do nothing but drive the 180 miles from Biscayne Bay to Key West, an all-new highway with 42 bridges connecting the dots of coralline-base tropical islands, you won't regret the trip. The Seven-Mile Bridge alone is an experience. And, if you first send for information about the Keys' incredible past, the trip will be even more fulfilling. No novel ever created has a more exciting plot or diverse cast of characters. It includes periods of fierce violence, alternating with times of peace and prosperity.

The island belonged to the violent Calusa Indians and Spanish explorers, who named the Keys *Los Martires*, meaning "suffering men," for their appearance. Then came pirates, whose difficulty navigating the treacherous reef-bound waters resulted in battles over sunken treasures. Next, the English held claim to the fragile land. This was followed by a boom period caused by sunken ship fortune hunters. In 1890, Key

West was the richest city in per capita income in the U.S. and had the largest Florida population. In 1912, Henry Flagler's 128-mile railroad brought more prosperity and residents. But the 1935 hurricane destroyed the railroad and much of the road linking the islands to the mainland. Proserity did not return until after World War II.

Today, those whose ancestors survived all this call themselves Conchs, after the beautiful shellfish which provides much of the protein in their diet.

Their isolation from the mainland, which continues today despite the highway, has resulted in the development of unique food traditions as "distinct" from the rest of the state as its history. Conch foods are a fascinating blend of Southern Cracker, zesty Latin and spicy Caribbean. Woven into the cuisine are tropical foods such as avocado, plantain, kumquat, guava, papaya, pineapple, coconut, and, of course, Key Limes.

But it is seafood, always abundant in these waters, that dictates most of the food habits and preferences. The yellowtail and red snapper, giant-size grouper, lobster, shrimp and stone crab vie for table-top honors. Oysters and clams are prevalent in the many raw bars, but conch is king. It is served grilled, ground in burgers, fried in batters, and raw.

As so many restaurants in the Keys are faithful to Conch food traditions, it is difficult to select just two to represent them. But as price is a primary consideration in the book, these do stand out.

The Lime Tree Bay Cafe, in the unincorporated town of Layton on Long Key, was a true discovery. Though a good deal less expensive than other well-known spots in the Middle Keys, the food is fresh, perfectly prepared to order and served in a tropically decorated atmosphere that seats about 30 in the dining area, a few more at the counter, and as many more in the two attached screened patios.

Owners Bill Stearns and Jim Schills opened the restaurant in early 1981 in the Lime Tree Bay Resort at Mile Marker 68½. Bill, who grew up in the Bahamas, had a life-long association with the business. His parents owned a restaurant in Bermuda. With their encouragement, he went to London to study wines. In 1974, he came to Florida, accepting a position with The Forge Restaurant in Miami to run their famed wine cellar. On vacation in the Keys, he and Jim were approached to open this restaurant on a Friday, accepted, and were serving breakfast Monday morning. Originally the Cafe served only breakfasts, specializing in a typical Keys breakfast of smoked fish and scrambled eggs with onions, peppers, cheese and bacon. They moved on to lunch hours, and now serve their individual and imaginative cuisine all day long.

From soup to dessert, all items are fresh and homemade. Chef Whitey, a graduate of the New York Culinary Institute, assists Bill and Jim in main course preparation.

Experts in fishing and netting, Bill and Jim serve their own catches, including tuna, brought in daily if weather permits. Bill says if they don't have fresh fish, they don't serve fish at all. The prevalent fish at the base of Whitey's dishes is dolphin in the summer and grouper in the winter. They smoke their own catch out back, when a recipe calls for it. They also net their own shrimp, which are kept fresh in a holding tank in the water just behind the restaurant. And they even grow their own Key Limes and bananas for their creative desserts.

Regular lunch and dinner menu items include raw or steamed oysters and clams, steamed or fried shrimp, smoked fish pate, conch fritters, fried conch and crab cakes. Sandwiches include Long Key Fish, Deep-Fried Catch on Grilled Rye with tartar, cole slaw and Swiss cheese; Conch Sandwich, Tuna Roll, and burgers. All of these are served with skin-on french fries or fresh cole slaw. Homemade soups include Oyster Stew, Clam Chowder, Fish Stew and Conch Chowder.

Dinners are ever changing, listed on the blackboard over the raw bar. They may include Chicken Meuniere, Shrimp a la Milton, Shrimp Tempura, Ham Steak, Chicken or Dolphin Almondine, Fish Escovitch. Dinners come with a fresh salad, potato or rice and vegetables, such as zucchini, squash, broccoli and mushrooms cooked fresh to order. The helpings are huge and the plates are enticingly garnished.

Desserts change each day as well but always include authentic Key Lime Pie and Strawberry Shortcake. Quite often, Bill has his own exotic fruit sherbets available.

Bill, Jim, Whitey and the entire crew (the original cast), are as natural as the Keys themselves. Bill, who has a reputation in the area for *never* wearing long pants, sets the example for the cafe's atmosphere of casual, friendly island dining. It's truly "come as you are," be as you are, and enjoy the picturesque waterfront setting for the Lime Tree Bay's best jewels of the sea.

How to get there: *Mile Marker 68½, Long Key. Take U.S. 1 to this marker. It's on the right side of the road about mid-way down the Keys, in the Lime Tree Bay Resort.*

While you're here: *The Lime Tree Bay Resort has a large display of exotic birds. It includes Amazon Parrots, Macaws, Toucans and Cockatoos. They also have an outdoor salt-water aquarium filled with brilliantly colored tropical fish caught just behind the restaurant. One of the best ways to enjoy the beauty of the Keys is to explore the crystal-clear waters surrounding them. Just next door to the restaurant you can rent a catamaran sailboat from Lime Tree Bay Boat Rental. You should also visit the nearby Shark World's Shark Institute to get a close-up look at Nurse, Bull, Tiger, Hammerhead and Lemon Sharks, along with tropical fish.*

FISH ESCOVITCH

4	fish fillets (grouper or snapper)
1	c. mayonnaise
2	T. horseradish
1	T. lemon juice (fresh squeezed)
2	pinches Old Bay seasoning
½	c. green pepper (diced)
½	c. onion (diced)
½	c. tomato (diced)

1. Place fish in single layer into shallow baking dish.
2. Mix together mayonnaise, horseradish, lemon juice, and Old Bay seasoning. Pour over top of fish.
3. Bake in oven at 400°F for 8-12 minutes, longer depending on thickness of fish.
4. Place raw green pepper, onion, and tomato over top of sauce. Place under broiler for several minutes, until golden brown.

Serves: 4
Preparation: 5 minutes
Cooking: 15 minutes

"A refreshing way to serve fish!"

— NOTES —

FISH ALMONDINE

4	fillets (use grouper, snapper, or even dolphin)
1	egg (beaten)
1	c. prepared bread crumbs
	butter for frying
¾	c. sliced blanched almonds (can use 'slivered' but not as colorful as 'sliced')
	fresh chopped parsley (garnish)
	juice of ½ lemon (garnish)

1. Dip fillets in beaten egg. Then dip into bread crumbs.
2. Heat butter in saute or frying pan,* add fillets. Cook until edges are brown.
3. Pour off butter. Cover fillets with almonds.
4. Bake in 400°F oven until you can smell the almonds — approximately 5 minutes baking time.
5. Top with parsley and lemon juice.

   *Use pan that is oven-proof, or remove handle.

Serves: 4
Preparation: 5 minutes
Cooking: 10-15 minutes

"The almonds give the fish a delightful taste and crunchy texture!"

— NOTES —

KEY LIME STRAWBERRY PINEAPPLE SHERBET

2 qts. whole milk
4½ c. sugar
1 fresh pineapple (cut into very small chunks)
1 pt. strawberries (cut into very small chunks)
juice from 18 Key Limes (may substitute
6 northern limes)
juice from 2 oranges
juice from 2 lemons
grated rind from 3 Key Limes (may substitute
1 northern lime)
garnish of orange and lemon rind
slices of lime
Optional: whipped cream

1. Mix milk and sugar well. Place in shallow dish.
   Put into freezer until ice forms on top (the semi-
   frozen stage).
2. Meanwhile, mix pineapple, strawberries, various
   juices, and rind from 3 limes in bowl. Stir several
   times while standing.
3. When milk mixture is ready, add fruit. Mix well.
   Return to freezer.
4. Serve when not quite frozen (The consistency of
   soft-serve ice cream).
5. Garnish with grated orange and lemon rind and a
   slice of lime. Whipped cream on top is optional!

   NOTE: Leftover sherbet can be kept well in freezer.
   It will freeze solid but when some is needed, allow
   to stand at room temperature until softened.

Makes: ½ gallon
Preparation: 30 minutes
Freezing: 2-3 hours for both steps

*"A fabulous dessert with a tangy taste that sits well after
a hearty meal!"*

Capt. Bob's Shrimp Dock

"Free beer tomorrow."   — The Conch philosophy

— Key West —

Just as exploration for sunken treasures led thousands to Key West to seek their fortunes in the 1800s, the same anticipation of discovering the island's 20th-century treasures leads thousands of tourists to explore its wide variety of gourmet restaurants, art and craft shops, unique clothing shops, old Victorian homes with gingerbread trim, museums and attractions.

The many restaurants in Key West feature the greatest of the island's treasures, its diverse cuisine combining the ethnic traditions of its residents, ancestors and native conchs. There are dozens of restaurants on the island that easily qualify to be a part of this book. But, recommendations of friends who often visit here, as well as locals, always included Capt. Bob's Shrimp Dock on their lists.

Captain Bob, whose land name is Robert Tradup, opened his seafood restaurant in 1971. Born and raised in New York

City, he followed a career with NASA in Washington, DC, after which he sought a place that would never be diseased with urban blight. He opened a restaurant in Alaska but wanted to find a warmer climate. The Keys' limited geographic growth potential, along with its distance from the mainland, made it the perfect spot. He arrived with his wife and children in 1967.

Capt. Bob's is located just off Duval next to the docks, which provide the freshest seafood for his dishes. The restaurant, which is quite spacious, is decorated "ship style" with fishing nets, wood-paneled walls, shipping and sea memorabilia, wood tables and captains' chairs.

The captain himself carries through the nautical theme with his own "old salt" appearance and manner that bring to mind portraits of Hemingway, sans pipe.

His menu, which varies slightly between lunch and dinner, is authentic "Conch Republic," the name locals have given their homeland. Appetizers include Clams or Oysters on the Half Shell, Oysters Rockefeller, Deviled Crab, Fried Clams, Conch Chowder and Conch Fritters. The chowder is Bob's own recipe, and aside from being very flavorful, contains more conch and vegetable chunks than many you may sample elsewhere in the Keys. The fritters are similar in flavor to others but have better texture from being made smaller in order to be fully cooked. This, too, is Bob's own recipe.

Lunch items include Fish and Chips, Shrimp Jambalaya, Shrimp Newburg, Lobster Newburg, Half Broiled Lobster Stuffed with Crab Meat, and the specialty of the house, Shrimp Steamed in Beer.

The dinner menu includes most of these same items priced no higher than lunch, but with several additions including Scallops, Swordfish, Red Snapper Almondine, catch-of-the-day, several platters, Crab Claws and Steaks.

Capt. Bob's is priced slightly higher than most other restaurants included in this book, but then, so are many of the eateries in Key West. The Shrimp Dock gives you more than your money's worth, however, with huge servings, quality, and freshness. There is also a children's and senior's menu to assist a family budget.

Despite his volume, Capt. Bob allows nothing to be prepared ahead of time except soups and desserts. Fish and shrimp arrive twice each day. Deep-fried items are breaded, not battered, so as not to hide the fresh flavor.

He not only serves authentic Key Lime pie, but also knows its history. He says the popular dessert was a story of "necessity is the mother of invention." Early spongers in the area were required to be out to sea for long periods of time as they harvested by pole, rather than diving. They could take only non-perishable items which included sweetened condensed milk. Key Limes grew wild on the offshore islands. They combined the two to make a Flan. Later, on the land, it was put into a crust. Bob cautions against Key Lime pie imitations. There should be no egg whites, no gelatin and certainly no green food coloring.

Capt. Bob's Shrimp Dock is a great place to get friendly with the natives, both the land and sea varieties.

How to get there: 908 Caroline Street, Key West. There is only one way to get to Key West, Hwy. 1. Once on the island, take a right on Roosevelt Boulevard to Duval Street. Make another right on Caroline Street (eight blocks) to address.

While you're here: It will take at least a week to see and do all there is on this relatively small island. For many people, favorites include shopping and touring the old gingerbread trimmed homes, which were built by ship builders with many similarities. You should also visit Mallory Square at sunset. The island comes alive with festivities every evening to celebrate the day's end, or perhaps the night's beginning. The island's many artists, musicians, storytellers and entertainers come down to the Square to display their talents.

Anglers should take advantage of the exciting fishing opportunities. Visit the Garrison Bight marina docks and rent a half or full day fishing adventure on Capt. Bill Hudson's Starr L. And while you are at this marina, have lunch or dinner at The Kangaroo's Pouch. It's a two-level houseboat, in one of the slips, that provides a novel experience in fresh seafood dining afloat.

CONCH CHOWDER

⅓   **c. onion (diced)**
2   **T. cooking oil**
3   **1 lb. cans potatoes (drained and diced)**
2   **t. Kitchen Bouquet**
2   **t. oregano**
1   **t. black pepper**
2   **t. salt**
1   **bay leaf**
2   **t. Accent**
½   **t. garlic powder**
2½   **lbs. conch (or may substitute clams. In Florida, purchase conch at your local seafood market.*)**
3-4   **stalks celery**
1-2   **large carrots**
⅓   **c. tomato paste**
¼   **c. green pepper (diced)**
3-4   **qts. water**

1. In large pot saute onion in oil. Add potatoes and seasonings.
2. Grind conch, celery, and carrots until fine. Add to pot along with tomato paste and green pepper.
3. Add 3-4 quarts water. Cook over medium-low heat for 4-5 hours (if using clams grind them alone and add 1 hour before serving).
4. Serve or cool if you have extra. (Make sure the soup is cool before refrigeration, otherwise the conch will sour.)

*If you'd like the name of a supplier from whom you can purchase conch, write us and we'll gladly furnish you with a list of suppliers.

Makes: 1½ gallons
Preparation: 20 minutes
Cooking: 5 hours

"A delicious blend of flavors causing aromas that will make your mouth water while it's cooking!"

CONCH FRITTERS

3   c. water
1   t. Accent
½   t. garlic powder
1   t. salt
½   t. black pepper
¾   t. oregano
4-6   c. self-rising flour
1   lb. conch meat (fresh ground or frozen —
       may substitute clams)
½   c. green pepper (diced)
       oil for frying

1.   Mix water and spices together.
2.   Add flour until drop consistency.
3.   Add remaining ingredients.
4.   Batter should be stiff enough to drop by teaspoon
     into oil heated to 350°F. Cook until brown.

Makes: 8-10 dozen
Preparation: 15 minutes
Cooking: 15-25 minutes

*"A pleasant delight to your taste buds.
You'll love conch!"*

— NOTES —

CAPT. BOB'S SHRIMP DOCK
KEY WEST

REAL KEY LIME PIE

5 **egg yolks**
1 **can sweetened condensed milk**
5 **oz. (scant ⅔ c.) Key Lime juice**
 graham cracker crust
 meringue or whipped cream, optional

1. In bowl blend egg yolks and milk.
2. Add lime juice — quickly while stirring.
3. Pour into crust.
4. Chill.
5. Add toppings, if desired.
   NOTE: If unable to get Key Lime juice use equal
   amounts of juice from fresh limes and
   lemons. Do **NOT** use bottled juice.

Serves: 6-8
Preparation: 5 minutes
Chill: 2-3 hours

"The world famous pie — straight from the area it was named for!"

— NOTES —

Lunch on Limoges

— Dade City —

Lunch on Limoges might be compared with a salmon swimming upstream — a restaurant following a path so different from the others that you wouldn't expect to find anything like it, least of all in rural Florida.

Dade City, 35 miles northeast of Tampa, is a quiet, country community of about 10,000 people. Those who aren't retirees make a living primarily from the 200 surrounding acres of citrus groves or from cattle raising. This area processes nearly one-fifth of all citrus fruits produced in Florida. A small youth population centers around St. Leo's College, a co-ed Catholic college just west of town, that is a most beautiful campus.

In the heart of downtown, a four-block strip of small businesses with a "Main Street" atmosphere, is Williams' Fashion Center. The center is an unusual and exciting combination of vogue fashions, direct from New York City, and nouvelle cuisine under one roof, a progressive and contemporary marketing concept that has caught on like a match in dry brush.

Williams' Fashions has been in co-owner Phil Williams' family since 1908. The elegant art deco building that houses the women's fashions and restaurant has belonged to the family since it was constructed in the '20s.

Though Phil was successful, and content, in running the women's wear segment of the center, his vast travels, and familiarity with New York's diverse cuisine, gave him an overwhelming urge to create a fashionable restaurant. He teamed up with Skip Mize, who shares his talent for people-pleasing, and began creating.

The resulting Lunch on Limoges is a step out of beat from other restaurants featured in this book but most assuredly gourmet, as much as Dade City is "underground."

Lunch on Limoges has uptown flair and pizzazz, combined with a genuine down-home personality. Phil and Skip created the name when they planned to serve their cuisine on Limoges china, a delicate porcelain variety made in Limoges, France, that carries a high-ticket price, too high for the kitchen casualties to be expected in any restaurant. But their alternate choice, clear-pink crystal table and stemware, placed on white linen tablecloths, accented by pink linen napkins and fresh flowers, is *tres chic*.

One key to Lunch on Limoges' success is the decor. Elegant but not pretentious, it is ever so lightly art deco combined with the warmth of linen, plants and cane chairs. The open kitchen invites customers to watch Skip and assistants create the unusual dishes. Waitresses carry through the nostalgic theme dressed in romantic period white lace and cotton dresses with long aprons. Fresh, exotic flowers — sometimes imported from Holland — are placed throughout the restaurant, both on tables and in huge arrangements in the open kitchen.

A second key draws from Phil and Skip's fashion merchandising experience, utilizing the same marketing techniques for the restaurant, with fresh promotions, special events, and an ever-changing "inventory." They believe restaurants should utilize fashion trends as much as clothing. For example, the day of the Royal British Wedding, they procured a large screen television and planned a special wedding feast. For the restaurant's anniversary, they held a week-long Mexican Fiesta with an appropriate menu. Quite often, fashions are modeled from their shop during the lunch hour.

And finally, the superb quality of the food assures the restaurant's success. Phil and Skip are constantly testing new recipes and following food trends.

Your meal will begin with miniature strawberry muffins, served warm in a linen-covered basket, accompanied by silver cups filled with butter, homemade marmalade, and pepper jelly. Try the Crab Meat Quiche, filled with large pieces of crab meat, fresh mushrooms, and green peppers, flavored with sherry and a variety of seasonings, and topped with a thick layer of cheddar. The slice is enormous, and the crust as tender as the filling. This entree includes a fresh fruit salad that looks as if it belongs on the cover of *Better Homes and Gardens*. It includes grapes, cantaloupe, apples, blueberries, strawberries, grapefruit, peaches hand-picked by Phil and Skip, and exotic star-shaped Chinese fruit, all soaked in white wine for two hours, then served with poppy seed dressing. The salad varies with season and whim, sometimes including kiwi fruit from Australia or fresh pineapple from California.

Or you can sample the Chicken Merangie, baked chicken in a tomato-base sauce with mushrooms, accented by basil, rosemary and oregano, smothered in Swiss cheese, and served over rice. It's served with a greens salad that is an assortment of lettuce leaves, zucchini, sunflower seeds, artichoke hearts, and black olives.

The Chicken Galentina is a work of art, particularly with the colorful garnish arrangements. The Galentina (a popular trend in food fashion) is chicken breasts pounded thin, with several repeating layers of herbs, bread crumbs, salami, and parsley. It is then rolled and baked, chilled and cut into attractively shaped pinwheel slices.

Other choices, which may vary, include Ham and Vegetable Quiche, Strawberry and Chicken Salad with Celery Soup, Turkey and Bacon Sandwich on Homemade Dill Bread, served with Poppy Seed Potato Salad. Desserts include Fresh Strawberry Torte and French Silk Pie.

Be sure to sample the tender croissants, served with meat and cheese filling or cream cheese and onion specially made by a Parisienne bakery in Orlando.

Skip and Phil continually experiment with unusual food combinations and seasonings. They grow their own New Zealand Spinach, a vine version that keeps itself up and out of the sand, so customers won't have the unpleasant experience of biting into hard granules. They have an Indian acquaintance who sends them exotic spices from her country. They use other little-known seasonings like nasturtium leaves, a type of cress. And, they invent their own recipes like their Herb Bread, and a Potato-Leek Casserole with Vegetable Pate.

Skip feels he owes it to their customers to always have something fresh and new on the menu. "I eat one meal while imagining the next," he says.

How to get there: 109 S. 7th Street, Dade City. Take Interstate 75 to Hwy. 52. Head east to U.S. 301, then north into downtown and take a right on 7th St. to address.

While you're here: If you are a woman and unable to travel to New York City to freshen up your wardrobe each season, Phil and Skip will bring New York to you. They personally select their exclusive inventory of vogue fashion apparel for women.

Take a drive through St. Leo's College. The picturesque setting will destroy any misconception that Florida is flat.

For you arbor lovers, the largest camphor trees in Central Florida can be viewed from West 54 near Wesley Chapel. And, if you arrive in the fall, during the third week of October, catch the International Rattlesnake Round-up in San Antonio. Stay & see a venom milking contest!

BROCCOLI MUSHROOM SOUP

1	c. leeks (sliced)
1	c. mushrooms (sliced)
3	T. butter
¼	c. flour
3	c. chicken broth
1	c. broccoli florets (chopped)
1	c. light cream
1	c. Swiss cheese (shredded)
2	eggs

1. In large saucepan, place leeks, mushrooms, and butter. Saute until tender (do not brown).
2. Add flour and stir until bubbly.
3. Remove from heat and gradually add chicken broth, stirring until mixed.
4. Return to heat and cook still stirring until thickened and smooth.
5. Add broccoli. Reduce. Simmer 15 minutes or until vegetables are tender.
6. Mix cream, Swiss cheese, and eggs in mixing bowl. Temper by adding a small amount of soup to the bowl until ingredients are warm, stirring constantly.
7. While stirring, slowly pour the tempered egg mixture into pot.
8. Simmer until heated through and cheese is thoroughly melted.

Serves: 8
Preparation: 15 minutes
Cooking: 35 minutes

"A delightful blending of flavors!"

POPPY SEED DRESSING

¾   c. sugar
1   c. vegetable oil
⅓   c. cider vinegar
1   T. onion juice *or* ⅛ t. onion (grated)
1   t. salt
1   t. dry mustard
1½ T. poppy seeds

1. Combine all ingredients, except poppy seeds in blender.
2. Process on high speed until well blended.
3. Stir in poppy seeds.
4. Chill thoroughly. Stir well before serving.

Yield: 1¾ cups
Preparation: 5 minutes
Chill: 2-3 hours

"Serve over bed of assorted greens and sliced radishes or over fresh fruit! Enjoy!"

— NOTES —

STRAWBERRY MUFFINS
(Use Food Processor)

1½ c. flour
½   c. chilled butter (cut into 6 pieces)
¾   c. sugar
1   t. baking soda
¼   t. salt
2   eggs
¼   c. milk
2   t. sherry
½   c. walnuts
1   c. fresh strawberries (cut up)

1. In food processor bowl use knife blade. Add the flour, butter, sugar, soda, and salt.
2. Process for 10 seconds.
3. In small bowl, combine eggs and milk. Beat well. Add mixture to other ingredients. Process 10-15 seconds.
4. Add sherry. Turn processor on. Then off quickly.
5. Add nuts. Process 10 seconds. Add strawberries. Process 10 seconds.
6. Bake in small muffin cup pans at 350°F for 10-12 minutes or until just light brown. (If using regular muffin cup pans, bake 18-20 minutes.)

Makes: 36 small muffins or 18 regular
Preparation: 5 minutes
Cooking: 20 minutes

"The easiest muffins you'll ever make!"

— NOTES —

HERB BREAD

1   pkg. dry yeast
¼   c. lukewarm water
1   t. light brown sugar
1   T. butter (melted)
1   c. cottage cheese
1½   T. light brown sugar
1   t. salt
¼   t. baking soda
2   t. dill seed*
2½   c. unbleached flour (sifted)
       melted butter
       salt

1. In small bowl, sprinkle yeast over water. Stir in 1 t. light brown sugar. Let this mixture rest for 10 minutes until it puffs and bubbles a little.
2. Meanwhile, in large saucepan, combine butter, cottage cheese, 1 T. light brown sugar, salt, and baking soda. Heat mixture until lukewarm.
3. Remove from heat and stir in yeast mixture.
4. Fold in dill seed.
5. Place flour in food processor bowl. Pour slowly into bowl the contents of saucepan. Flour will absorb liquid. Mix until a stiff mass.
6. Let rise 1 hour in warm place. Cover lightly with moist towel.
7. Turn dough out on lightly floured board and knead for a few minutes.
8. Turn into 5x9″ loaf pan. Let rise 30-40 minutes or until it has risen above rim of pan.
9. Bake in oven preheated to 350°F for 40-45 minutes.
10. Brush top with butter and sprinkle with salt.

*To substitute for dill seed use fennel or caraway seeds, basil, tarragon, or oregano.

Makes: 5x9″ loaf
Preparation: 2 hours
Cooking: 45 minutes

"A most unusual taste — try with cream cheese lovingly spread on slices!"

— NOTES —

— NOTES —

The Little Inn Restaurant

— Homosassa Springs —

As the most outstanding feature of The Little Inn in Homosassa Springs is the price, it is quite appropriate that the names of the owners are Bob and Betty Price.

They are also responsible for the comfort of their restaurant. Billboards announcing your proximity to The Little Inn advertise the friendly atmosphere. That's not an unusual claim, but in this case, it is particularly true.

The best testimony to the quality of a restaurant are its regulars. Go there a few minutes before 11, when the doors open, and talk with the customers waiting outside. One elderly couple says they stop for lunch at least three times a week, always early as it is a long wait at lunch time. They rave about Betty Price who, in her late twenties, is dearly loved by the primarily retired population of the area. When she drives up, there are smiles on all faces awaiting her arrival.

The Little Inn, in existence two years, has 21 tables seating about 62 customers, in an atmosphere of greenery and sunny exposure.

Nearly 20 menu selections are offered any time of day, along with the same number of dinner selections, a dozen lunch specials, several daily specials, pasta entrees, soup, salads, sandwiches and desserts. Altogether you can choose from more than 70 entree selections!

Betty was raised on a farm in Wisconsin and is well accustomed to the benefits of home cooking, hiring only the best cooks and waitresses. The rule of the house is "Everybody smile!"

But Betty feels it is her customers who deserve the credit for the quality of The Little Inn. "We always ask our customers if the food was right, and they tell us," she says. "If we run out of an ingredient and substitute, they know the difference. If we try a different brand of an ingredient, they know that, too."

Her intimacy with her customers has its drawbacks though. "I get emotionally involved with the customers. And, as many are elderly, I have a hard time when they pass away."

One of her regulars whom she calls "Grandma" walks a full mile to the restaurant every day. Another, an 86-year-old man who lives across the street, watches from the window every day for a slack time and walks over for his daily meal.

It's no coincidence that many of the regular customers are elderly. Aside from the population make-up of the area, the prices are well within the range for a fixed income.

For example, a Pepper Steak Dinner served with potatoes, gravy, vegetable and garlic bread costs only a few dollars. For dinner, a Sauteed Fresh Scallop Dinner served with homemade soup, vegetable, hush puppies and house bread is also modestly priced.

Entree favorites include Shrimp Creole and Chicken Parmigian. The honey-lime sauce served over fresh fruit is a treat. You should also sample the peanut butter pie and homemade ice cream...yes, homemade! Apple pie with cinnamon sauce is a great surprise for apple pie lovers.

Though The Little Inn is closed on Mondays, it stays open for holidays. Because many of the customers call the restaurant "home," Bob and Betty don't turn them away on holidays when it's most important to see a friendly face. They decorate the restaurant in the theme of the day and serve a special menu.

Even before noon, every table in the restaurant will be filled with diners. The restaurant is even more popular in the evening, serving more than 250 over the dinner hour. Hungry faces are always standing by, eagerly awaiting a table.

What better testimony for the excellence of an underground gourmet restaurant?

How to get there: U.S. 19, just off the main traffic light in Homosassa Springs. Closed Monday.

While you're here: If you are into roughing it a little, the Turtle Creek Campground is a natural pleasure to share with your family or friends. Every Saturday night you can take part in a real Florida country hoe-down, complete with a country meal. It's all outdoors in an open pavilion surrounded by pines and cypress. Bring a musical instrument, if you play one. The fun begins around 8. The campground is located on Turtle Creek (a feeder to the Homosassa River) on S.R. 490 a few miles west of Hwy. 19. Call for reservations.

As the Turtle Creek camp song says (and everyone knows it before they leave), "Escape to the country, lose those city blues. Campfires and music, forget those Union dues."

SPLIT-PEA SOUP
(Allow Peas to Soak Overnight)

1	c. split peas
2-4	c. water
1	carrot (diced)
1	small onion (diced)
	ham bone
½	t. celery salt
½	t. garlic powder
	salt and pepper to taste
3	c. milk

1. Wash peas several times then place them in pan with water and allow to soak overnight.
2. The next day add carrot, onion, and ham bone. Cook over medium heat until it boils. Simmer uncovered until peas are tender, about 1½ hours.
3. Remove ham bone and press the material through a seive. Return to pot with liquid they were cooked in. Add seasonings, milk, and any meat pieces from bone.
4. Heat through, stirring to thicken. Serve hot.

Serves: 4-6
Preparation: Soak overnight/10 minutes
Cooking: 2-3 hours

"Lip-smacking good with cornbread!"

— NOTES —

HONEY-LIME DRESSING

1   c. mayonnaise
½   c. honey
¾   t. paprika
1   t. celery seed
2-3 T. lime juice
1   drop green food coloring
1   20-oz. package frozen mixed fruit (or 1½ c. mixed fresh fruit)

1. Mix all ingredients together and refrigerate.
2. Pour over defrosted fruit. Serve.

Serves: 4
Preparation: 5 minutes
Chill: 2-3 hours

"A nice, cool and refreshing dessert!"

— NOTES —

CHICKEN PARMIGIAN

2	whole chicken breasts, split and de-boned
4	eggs (whipped)
½	c. bread crumbs
½	c. self-rising flour
1	T. garlic powder
½	t. paprika
1	t. white pepper
1	t. salt
4	slices Provolone cheese
2	c. spaghetti sauce (canned or homemade)

1. Blend bread crumbs, flour, and all seasonings together on a large dinner plate. Dip each chicken breast half into eggs, then into coating mix on plate.
2. Place chicken in a 5x7" baking dish. Bake at 350°F for 30 minutes or until done.
3. Place 1 chicken breast half on each dinner plate. Cover each with 1 slice Provolone cheese and ½ cup spaghetti sauce. Return plates to oven (or microwave) until cheese melts.

Serves: 4
Preparation: 15 minutes
Cooking: 30 minutes

"The coating mix for the chicken is great!... the extra can be refrigerated in a plastic bag for future use... Umm!"

— NOTES —

— NOTES —

The Blueberry Patch, Brooksville, Florida

P. STOCKEY

The Blueberry Patch

— Brooksville —

In keeping with the restful impression of the Brooksville area, the Blueberry Patch is a charming "tea room" occupying a restored home of the late 1800s. Brooksville is a quiet community in West Central Florida, approximately 40 miles north of Tampa, an ideal blend of rustic surroundings and city convenience. Brooksville also enjoys the rare amenity of altitude. At 175 feet above sea level, it is one of the highest points in Florida, and no doubt a destination goal in many a family's hurricane escape plans. The altitude contributes to a striking contrast in vegetation and terrain from that of nearby coastal communities.

The city grew from a combination of two communities, Melendez and Pierceville, which merged in the mid-1800s. One of the families that "remembers when" now owns The Blueberry Patch, one of the finest, most unusual restaurants in the area.

Each of the high-ceiling rooms in the 85-year-old house has been furnished with intimate table and seating arrangements, yet retains a homespun Early American atmosphere in the decor. White ruffled cafe curtains, checkered tablecloths with white linen coverlets, oak floors, floral print wallpaper and dozens of antique accents create a most pleasant, natural and cheery climate for dining. It's like going to a relative's house for a holiday meal — it's special, and you're a guest, but you belong and feel at home.

Each of the six dining rooms (seating no more than 20 in any one) has a special name referring to the theme of the room. There are the Rose Room, the Tea Room, the Garden Room, the Basket Room, the Porch, and the Cupboard Room, the favorite of owners Pug Swain, Mary Jernigan and their mother, Cassie Grubs.

This room seats just six people, two at each of three tables. According to Mary, the people seated at these tables always leave knowing one another, and the intimacy of the room has produced many new friendships.

The three owners, all born and raised in Brooksville and now in their fourth generation of family residency, are an essential part of the restaurant's success.

As you might expect, the food is as genuine as the atmosphere and hostesses. There are no fried foods on the menu, and everything listed is made from scratch. The menus are adorable...a blue etching of the house on a notecard-size booklet, with pages that read like an invitation to a party.

French Onion and Cream of Broccoli soups are your first invitation. The French Onion is the real thing with the type of cheese that *longs* to remain on the soup, spanning the gap between mouth and bowl. And, in keeping with the theme of intimacy, the Greek and Spinach Salads are served only for two.

Entree choices vary slightly between lunch and dinner; the prices more so. Selections include Chicken Elegante (chicken in a sherry, mushroom sauce served over wild rice), Ham Steak, Pepper Steak, Broccoli Casserole, Salmon Loaf and Fiesta Shrimp (a gorgeous concoction of shrimp sauce with green onion, mushroom and bell peppers over rice). But the star of this show is Beef Bourguignon, a classic French Stew of tender beef, onions and mushrooms in a dark, rich wine sauce served over rice. Make it for some special company — you'll razzle-dazzle 'em! Hot Chicken Souffle, one of the many daily specials, has the flavor of chicken salad but is enriched by layers of bread, cheese and mushroom sauce.

Be sure to save room for the dessert menu. Choices include Blueberry Cheesecake, Coconut and Chocolate Sour Cream

Cakes, Kentucky Derby Pie (pecan pie with chocolate chips and bourbon) and Silk Pies (layers of cream cheese, pecans and silky vanilla filling topped with fruit). If you're still reading, you may have gained five pounds already!

The Porch, a sunny dining room, also features a nook of handmade gifts at very reasonable prices.

How to get there: 414 East Liberty Street, Brooksville. Take U.S. 41 into Brooksville to the intersection of 41 and S.R. 50, just 2 blocks west of Roger's Christmas House.

While you're here: Visit Brooksville in February when the dogwoods and azaleas are in full bloom. The best view is from University of South Florida's Conference Hill or Chinsegut Hill, a beautiful site for a picnic. And, Christmas can be any day of the year at Roger's Christmas House. An entire home, just two blocks from the Blueberry Patch, has been transformed into a magical Christmas fantasy. Browsers are welcome.

HOT CHICKEN SALAD SOUFFLE
(Allow to Refrigerate Overnight)

6   slices white bread
2½-3 lb. whole chicken (or 2 c. diced cooked chicken)
1   stalk celery (chopped) — cook with whole chicken
1   small onion (chopped)
     salt to taste
½   c. celery (finely chopped)
½   c. onion (finely chopped)
½   c. green pepper (finely chopped)
½   c. salad dressing
½   c. cheddar cheese (shredded)
3   slightly beaten eggs
1½ c. milk
1   can cream of mushroom soup

1. Cook whole chicken with celery, onion, salt and enough water to halfway cover chicken. Cook until done, turning over halfway through cooking. Cool and dice 2 c. chicken.
2. Trim crusts from bread slices (save for future use) and place trimmed bread in bottom of 9 x 13″ baking dish.
3. Combine the chicken, finely chopped celery, onion and green pepper with the salad dressing. Carefully spread oven bread slices.
4. Crumb or cube the reserved crusts and use as topping over chicken mixture. Sprinkle cheese over crusts.
5. Mix eggs and milk together. Pour over all ingredients in baking dish.
6. Refrigerate overnight.
7. Before baking, spoon can of soup over top and bake in 350 °F over for 1 hour.

Serves: 6-8
Preparation: 30 minutes — 1 hour
Cooking: 1 hour

"Excellent for buffet entertaining! Don't plan on leftovers — there won't be any!!"

LEMON CLOUD PIE

8   oz. package cream cheese
1   c. powdered sugar
8   oz. container whipped topping (Cool Whip)
1   baked pie shell (or use butter-flavored 'ready-crust')
1   can lemon pie filling
   Cool Whip for topping

1. Soften cream cheese. Add powdered sugar and whip together.
2. Fold whipped topping into cream cheese mixture.
3. Layer cream cheese mixture in bottom of pie shell. Place lemon pie filling on top.
4. Refrigerate for 3-4 hours. Top each serving with Cool Whip, if desired.

Serves: 8
Preparation: 15 minutes
Chill: 3-4 hours

"Very, very easy! Elegant results...perfect for summer in Florida. No oven required."

— NOTES —

— NOTES —

The Four B's Restaurant

— Ocala —

Ocala is a beautiful community in the heart of north-central Florida. The terrain is rolling and woodsy, and is the nation's largest breeding and training center for thoroughbred horses. (Bet you thought that was Kentucky's claim, didn't you?) The Ocala National Forest is a fabulous area for a weekend's journey from either coast. Camping areas are scattered throughout. They are the rustic type (by today's standards) that allow you a comfortable margin of privacy. And, unlike many camping grounds in this state, you won't be the only one with a tent.

On your way through town, The Four B's Restaurant is a "must" rest stop. You can fill up for the weekend on the portions of "country fixin's" you'll find here. Barbara and son Marc Leuchtman took over the 31-year-old restaurant a few years ago but kept the same basic menu, adding a number of special creations of their own which they had perfected by their 11 years in the business.

The decor of the 150-seat (two separate rooms) restaurant is not particularly unusual, but the food *is* most certainly. It's all down-home country cooking served in hungry-size portions.

Though the bacon-wrapped filet mignon steaks in four custom-tailored sizes are the house specialty, have someone in your party order the king-cut prime rib. You won't believe the size until you see it — two pounds plus and at least 3″ high.

In addition to several steak selections, the menu features Baked Chicken, Barbecued Ribs, Italian entrees, a wide range of reasonably priced seafood, several combination dinners, and sandwiches. A "Super Salad" is topped with a full quarter of a chicken, ham, cheese and lots of extras.

A "Young'uns Under 12" menu and a "Seniors Over 65" menu make The Four B's a popular spot for old-fashioned family get-togethers. Both menus feature a variety of entrees, with all the "fixin's," at even lower prices than the regular menu.

Though the restaurant doesn't open until 4 p.m., Barbara and Marc get the ovens going at sunrise. Steaks are hand-cut from specially ordered Midwest beef. Their steaks are so popular that The Four B's does a brisk business in wholesale meat sales as well.

All dinners are served with a choice of extras including homemade soup (Clam Chowder, Split Pea Barley and Creamy Broccoli are local favorites), homemade cole slaw, salad with their extra-special house dressing, fries or baked potato, rice pilaf, and a choice of veggies and rolls including their homemade muffins.

The baked potatoes aren't just your ordinary cooked spuds. They're a meal in themselves. The over-sized potatoes are baked, then scooped out, mashed and combined with butter and seasonings. Then the skins are re-stuffed and baked again. They're attractively prepared and weigh in around two pounds, measuring about 7″ long by 5″ high. They're called "mountain high."

If you still have room for dessert, Mud Pie, Key Lime Pie (the real thing, yellow), homemade pudding, cheesecake, pies and cakes are all made fresh daily.

The Four B's also offers an excellent wine selection for this type of restaurant, along with beer and house specialty cocktails. Sunday's popular buffet, including at least ten entrees (with Chicken and Dumplings ordered most often), brings customers from miles around. An early dinner here, and you'll *have* to make Sunday a day of rest!

How to get there: *4700 South Pine Avenue, Ocala. From I-75 (north or southbound) take the Hwy. 200 exit eastbound to Pine Avenue (SR 441-27-301). Turn right (south) four miles south of city limits.*

While you're here: *Hit the Ocala National Forest for the weekend and enjoy a part of Florida as exciting as sand between your toes. Or, for some "fast lane" entertainment, Six Gun Territory is a popular attraction. The Old Western Town, with special shows and rides, is located on Florida 40 between Ocala and Silver Springs.*

— NOTES —

HOT AND SPICY HOUSE DRESSING

2	c. catsup
1	T. sugar
1	t. fresh garlic (minced, in jar)
1	t. salt
1	t. black pepper
1	T. Worcestershire sauce
1	T. vinegar
½	t. paprika

1. Combine all ingredients in bowl and blend well.
2. Pour into quart jar and refrigerate until ready to use (refrigerate at least 4 hours).

Yield: 1½ pints
Preparation: 5 minutes
Chill: 4 hours (minimum)

"This lives up to its name!"

— NOTES —

FOUR B'S MUFFINS

1½ c. flour
2   t. baking powder
¼   t. salt
⅓   c. butter or margarine
½   c. milk
1   egg (beaten)
¼   c. sugar
1   c. carrots (finely grated)
½   t. pumpkin pie spice

1. Sift together flour, baking powder, salt into bowl. Cut in butter until it resembles coarse oatmeal.
2. Combine milk, egg, and sugar in smaller bowl. Pour into dry ingredients.
3. Add carrots and pumpkin pie spice. Mix until **just** moist (to overmix results in unrisen muffins).
4. Place in greased muffin pans.
5. Bake in 350°F oven for 20-30 minutes.

Makes: 1 dozen
Preparation: 15 minutes
Cooking: 30 minutes

"Very aromatic — good blend of flavors!"

— NOTES —

Palma Maria Restaurant

— Casselberry —

Philadelphia mourned the loss of Pete and Mary Rosinola. The paper there dedicated a full page of appreciation to them on the day of their departure. But what is Philadelphia's loss is Florida's gain.

The Rosinola family, who are also credited with introducing the Hoagie to Allentown, ran the Palma Maria Restaurant in Tamaqua, Pennsylvania for 30 years. Their customers would drive long distances to enjoy a full evening of feasting on Pete's own version of Italian cooking, influenced by Sicilian, Piedmontese and Neapolitan cuisine.

His typical 10-course meals, which would take no fewer than four hours to consume, would begin with Crab Soup and Court Bouillon, followed by Antipasto. Then came Quiche and Eggplant Shellbourn (fresh spinach, mushrooms, scallions, pignolia nuts and eggplant, sauteed and spooned into the eggplant shell and topped with cheese). Flounder Francaise, Veal Marsala, and White Pizza (a Rosinola original made with shallots, herbs, olive oil and mozzarella) would come next. Then Pete's Lasagna, which uses no tomato sauce and rises like a souffle. If you were still able to eat, you would then choose from several of Pete's elegant desserts.

Pete's feasts carried an appropriate price tag, and attracted clientele who could afford it. Mary says the restaurant was graced with stardom on several occasions, including a few visits from John Voight.

A particularly frustrating winter led Pete to a quick decision to move to Florida. Mary says there was no time even to discuss the move. So the Rosinola family headed south, reopening the Palma Maria Restaurant in Casselberry, just a few miles north of Orlando. The name of the restaurant was derived from his daughter Palma, who was born on Palm Sunday, his wife Mary Ann, and another daughter, Ann Marie.

Pete retained many of the same menu items, including his famous feast which included seven courses and a bottle of wine. But much to his dismay, he discovered that many Floridians are not gifted with voluminous appetites. For every customer who went the distance, two couldn't. Mary concludes that it is probably the heat and the slower pace of living in this state. So the feasts were dropped, and a deli sandwich menu replaced the gourmet selections.

Pete was frustrated, though, not being able to prepare his gourmet dishes. The menu is now somewhere in between the two extremes, and Orlando accepts Palma Maria with open arms.

The restaurant is intimate and attractive, yet casual enough for typical Sunbelt attire. Pete's cooking is definitely all his own, a mixture of Italian and French. Everything is prepared from scratch, right down to the pasta, which is angel hair thin.

Palma's dinner menu includes Linguine with Clam Sauce, Spaghetti with Sausage, Fettucini Alfredo, Veal Piccata, Eggplant Florentine, Eggplant Parmesan, Chicken Marsala and Baked Flounder with Crab Meat. You can also select the Soup of the Day, Mushroom Florentine, Quiche, Eggplant Shellbourn, or an Arugula Salad for an appetizer. For dessert, try a slice of peanut butter pie, cheesecake or Pete's famous cannoli (a delicate shell filled with ricotta, custard and lemon, topped with whipping cream and melted chocolate). If you call ahead, Pete will make up one of his fabulous Stromboli, a pastry filled with dozens of layers of Italian meats, cheeses and herbs.

Though he doesn't advertise pizza on the menu and doesn't

consider himself a pizza cook, his is outstanding. The difference is in the crust. It's high but very light with a thin, outside crispy layer — so delicious you could eat an entire crust without anything on it. The toppings are fresh and juicy, with flavorful cheeses and Pete's own homemade sausage.

Palma Maria — don't miss it!

How to get there: 1015 E. Hwy. 436, Casselberry, Florida. Take Interstate 4 to Hwy. 436. Go east to the address. The restaurant is located in Summit Plaza, a shopping strip on the south side of the highway. Open for dinner, Tuesday through Saturday.

While you're here: Though an attempt has been made to stay away from typical tourist attractions , the attractions that have put Orlando on the map are those that few ever get their fill of. Orlando lets everyone know everything there is to do. Be sure to see Disney World, enjoy the excellent cuisine at the Walt Disney World Village restaurants in Lake Buena Vista. And don't forget Circus World, Sea World and the numerous excellent attractions. Watch the billboards, the hotel brochure racks, the newspaper and the sky (advertising space is crowded overhead in Orlando).

STUFFED FRESH ARTICHOKES

4	large globe artichokes
2-3	c. water
1	t. salt
1	T. lemon juice

— FILLING —

½	c. fresh white bread crumbs
2	T. fresh parsley (chopped)
1-2	cloves garlic (crushed)
	salt and pepper to taste
¾	c. Parmesan cheese
¾	c. fresh mushrooms (chopped) OR
	¾ c. crab meat OR
	2 hard boiled eggs (chopped)
	olive oil
	water for steaming

1. Cut off 1″ across top of artichokes and across bottom stem so they will sit flat in pan. Cut off tips of leaves to remove spines. Wash thoroughly.
2. In deep saucepan combine water, salt, and lemon juice. Bring to boil. Stand artichokes in pan. Cover and cook until barely tender (25-35 min.)
3. Drain. Discard some of the inner leaves and scoop out the hairy center "choke" with a teaspoon.

— FILLING —

4. Mix all ingredients together with just enough olive oil to moisten and hold ingredients together.
5. Spread artichoke leaves. Place ¼ of filling in each artichoke.
6. Place filled artichokes in shallow baking dish. Tie string around leaves to hold together. Add ½″ water to bottom of dish.
7. Sprinkle a little olive oil on top of each artichoke.

8.   Cover pan tightly with aluminum foil. Bake in
     350°F. oven for 30-45 minutes, until tender.

Serves: 4
Preparation: 20 minutes
Cooking: 35/45 minutes

"You'll want to eat all 4 yourself ... a luscious treat."

— NOTES —

PALMA MARIA
ORLANDO

ORANGE SALAD

---

1   **orange**
1   **T. olive oil**
    fresh ground black pepper
    fresh mint leaves (chopped) or dried,
    crushed leaves

1. Pare orange. Slice across in ⅛-¼" slices.
2. Arrange slices on salad plate. Sprinkle olive oil over top, then pepper and mint leaves.
3. Let stand 5 minutes. Serve immediately or refrigerate. (Best if refrigerated!)

Serves: 1
Preparation: 5 minutes
Chill: 30 minutes

"This looks delightful on a leaf of escarole or endive and tastes out of this world!"

— NOTES —

Mama Lo's

She riseth also while it is yet night, and giveth meat to her household...

Give her the fruit of her hands; and let her own works praise her in the gates.

— Proverbs 31:15 and 31

— Gainesville —

Gainesville, in the north-central region of Florida, is an oasis of life surrounded by flat, sandy country, scrub oak and pine, dotted with clear, sandy-bottom lakes, and the home of famed Florida sinkholes. Sinkholes are ever-opening pockets of land which fill with rain-brought water, immediately followed by alligators. Hence, "Gator Country," the nickname for the area.

Gators and University of Florida students make up the greatest percentage of Gainesville's population. And, as birds of a feather flock together, the Gator has become the U of F mascot, and symbol of the area. The relationship of the two is quite symbolic of the community. Gators are a long-lived animal, usually reaching the half-century mark. Students are short-lived mammals, with any luck, ceasing their status within four years.

That is Gainesville...a blend of young and old, of New South and Old South. And, nothing in Gainesville more perfectly exemplifies that blend than Mama Lo's.

Lorine Alexander (Mama Lo) has been feeding Gainesville students and the "locals" for more than 16 years. Her mother and grandmother did so before her. The restaurant is more than a business to her — cooking is her life.

Mama Lo arrives at her small restaurant, with seating for 35, at 6 a.m. She works a 15-hour day, every day, leaving at 9 p.m. Her first duty is to decide what she will prepare that day. Then she writes out eight menus, by hand, on notebook paper, one for each table. Tax is added to each menu item to make things easy on her help.

Next she starts the incredible task of cooking at least 15 main courses, all the trimmings, from 15 to 20 vegetable dishes (fresh from her own garden in the country), and homemade pies and cakes that are tantalizingly set out to cool just inches from your table.

Most of us would find it difficult to prepare this quantity of food lovingly, single-handedly. Mama Lo's kitchen is no larger than your own, but she has a system. She must, in order to prepare the equivalent of 10 to 20 Thanksgiving dinners each morning.

On an average day, Mama Lo sends 200 happily stuffed customers out the door during the lunch hours alone and more at dinner. Though she isn't officially open for breakfast, she says, "If somebody comes in real hungry and asks me, I'll cook 'em up something."

Mama Lo's cooking is beyond description. It's all from scratch, from time-tested recipes she carries with her in her head. The portions are huge and the prices ridiculously low. A main dish comes with three side dish choices from more than a dozen, including fresh okra and tomato, collard greens, baked apple, candied yams, blackeyed peas and Mama Lo's famous Broccoli and Eggplant Casseroles.

Popular main dish choices are Barbecued Ribs, Roast Beef, Chicken or Turkey with Dressing, Smoked Sausage and Yams, and Stuffed Bell Peppers. Mama Lo also offers a tasty Southern dish, "Chitlins" (pig's "insides") though she confesses she hates to make them.

All dinners plus extras are most modestly priced. It's no wonder Mama Lo feeds so many college students. So, don't worry Mom, your kids are eating right at Mama's.

Mama Lo is herself the kind of woman who could make a career woman wonder if she is doing the right thing. She's everything that "Miz Jiffy" and "Miz Martha White" aren't. She's some lady!

How to get there: 618 N.W. 6th Street. From I-75 take the Archer Road Exit (Hwy. 24) east to 13th Street. Head north to 5th Avenue (past U of F campus). Turn right to N.W. 6th Street, then left one block. Mama Lo's is a white building right across from the police station and next to the church.

While you're here: Visit the University of Florida. It is a beautiful campus that destroys the myth that Florida caters only to the elderly. The University Gallery is a fascinating experience. And, if you're lucky, you might catch a U of F football game. The Gators are great!

Marjorie Kinnan Rawlings State Museum and Park is just 21 miles south of Gainesville on SR 325. The 125-acre park is a beautiful, historic monument to the famous Florida author of such novels as Pulitzer prize-winning The Yearling, Cross Creek *and* Golden Apples.

COLLARD GREENS

1   **bunch collard greens**
1   **T. shortening (Crisco)**
½   **T. butter**
½   **c. water**
1   **T. sugar**
1   **T. butter**
    salt and pepper to taste

1. Wash collard greens 3-4 times in running water until water runs clear. Then wash several more times to be sure they are clean (this is the secret to success as collards are **very** sandy!).
2. Chop collards very fine.
3. Heat shortening and butter until brown. Add collards and water.
4. Simmer for 1 hour. Watch so the pot doesn't go dry.
5. Add rest of ingredients. Serve.

Serves: 2-4
Preparation: 15 minutes
Cooking: 1½ hours

"Collards are a headless variety of cabbage that are rich in iron. Their appearance is similar to spinach but the flavor is unique. Their proper preparation is critical to maintain proper flavor!"

— NOTES —

STUFFED BELL PEPPERS

6	large, whole green peppers
1	lb. lean ground beef
½	onion (chopped)
½	c. ketchup
1	c. cooked rice (long grain white)
½	stalk celery (chopped)
	several dashes Worcestershire sauce
	salt and pepper to taste

— BROWN GRAVY —

2	c. water
4	T. butter
2	T. beef base (instant bouillon)
¼	t. garlic powder
4	T. cornstarch in ¼ c. water

1. Cut off ½-inch of peppers at stem end. Discard center stem. Chop remaining tops. Clean out peppers of seeds and pulp.
2. Combine chopped pepper with all remaining ingredients, mix well. Stuff into prepared peppers.
3. Place stuffed peppers in 9 x 11″ aluminum pan with 1 cup water in bottom. Cover with aluminum foil.
4. Bake in 350°F. oven for 30 minutes. Cover with brown gravy and serve.

— BROWN GRAVY —

5. Place all ingredients, except corn starch and water mixture in sauce pan and bring to rapid boil.
6. Reduce heat and add cornstarch and water mixture. Heat until gravy reaches a thick consistency.

Serves: 6
Preparation: 15 minutes
Cooking: 30 minutes/15 minutes

"The brown gravy adds a nice touch to an old favorite."

BROCCOLI CASSEROLE

1	bunch broccoli, peeled and chopped
5	slices day old white bread, cut in cubes
5	eggs
¼	c. milk
4	T. butter
1	c. grated sharp cheddar cheese
1	t. salt
4	T. sugar

1. Lightly grease a 9 x 11" baking dish (or use pan with non-stick finish).
2. Place bread cubes in bottom of dish. Place broccoli on top of cubes.
3. Thoroughly mix together remaining ingredients. Pour over broccoli and bread.
4. Cover with aluminum foil. Bake for 35 minutes in 350°F oven.

Serves: 6
Preparation: 20 minutes
Cooking: 35 minutes

"A very different taste for broccoli."

— NOTES —

Malaga Street Depot

— St. Augustine —

Finding out about Malaga Street Depot is like discovering a pot of gold at the end of the rainbow, only more difficult. You won't find it in any of the thousands of tour guides, tourist magazines, or "what to see and do" newspapers found everywhere and anywhere in this city and you won't find it advertised in the newspaper. In fact, the only way to find it is to follow a local resident whom you think might be heading out for breakfast.

Ned (Nathan) Pollack, who is also the chef, opened his restaurant in 1980. That was a very good year for restaurants in St. Augustine. Ned has been in the business all his life, owning his own restaurant since 1975. Originally from New Jersey, he owned Chickalini's Pasta Palace in Ohio before coming to St. Augustine. But Malaga Street Depot isn't anything like his pasta palace, quite intentionally.

Here, the egg comes before the chicken. In fact, the egg gets top billing on this menu. No one makes an egg "come out of its shell" like Ned. It's not just what he puts on top of his unusual egg entrees but what he puts into the mixture itself. With an unpretentious mass of yolks and whites, he creates fabulous meals that would hold their own in a steak vs. egg battle any day.

There are nine omelet choices, eggs "the way you like them," and five specialty choices which include Eggs Lorraine (an omelet topped with spinach, Swiss cheese, bacon, onions and sour cream), Eggs Benedict, Fritata (an omelet topped with zucchini, onion, peppers, potato, Provolone and Parmesan cheese), and Eggs Classical (scrambled eggs with onion, garlic, spinach, ham and Hollandaise sauce on an english muffin). Ned allows himself the freedom of substituting or adding ingredients based on season and whim by a disclaimer stating such on the menu. For example, my Fritata was given a bonus ingredient of asparagus.

There is also a sizable selection of salads and sandwiches, chalkboard specials, orange whole wheat hotcakes, crepes and homemade soups. Oddly enough, there are also four Mexican entrees, two of which feature Ned's "eggstra" touch. Huevos Rancheros is a tortilla topped with refried beans, two eggs, picante sauce and cheese. Breakfast Tacos are refried beans, peppers, onions and scrambled eggs rolled in a tortilla with picante sauce and cheese.

Nearly all of the entree selections include homefries and muffins, which are dishes "extraordinaire" in themselves. The homemade wholewheat oatmeal muffins are not particularly exciting on their own, but when topped with apple butter (there is a container on each table), their flavor and texture come alive.

The homefries, with the skins left on, are perfectly fried, brown and crunchy on the outside, tender and not greasy inside. They're seasoned in such a way that you let the second bite stay in your mouth awhile, to let your taste buds have a shot at figuring out just what makes them so different. You'll find yourself doing this with all his dishes.

It is Ned's preoccupation with seasonings that makes his restaurant so spectacular. You will first notice the difference when you walk in. The aroma is quite different from any other restaurant, as Ned is always experimenting with herbs and spices. His discriminating selection and use make his egg dishes like a great mystery novel...you don't always know what is going on, but you love every minute of it.

Even a seasoning expert could be completely stumped by

Ned's "secret" spicing. You might detect dill weed, which does wonderful things for eggs. But the more exotic primary flavors turn out to be Cilantro and Paprika Weiss special-ordered from New York.

Ned's love of herbs is visually confirmed on the walls of his restaurant. Intermingled with several excellent paintings by local artists are actual herb plants, preserved and box-framed.

The restaurant seats approximately 30 customers at tables and several more at bar stools, providing a full view of Ned's "one-man-band" kitchen. The entire cooked-to-order menu is prepared at one stove. But despite the crowd, your order arrives in just minutes. It's no wonder Ned dresses in shorts and tennis shoes, as do the waitresses.

Though Malaga Street Depot, so named from the address and neighboring bus depot, is open for breakfast and lunch only, the sizable portions of fabulous egg dishes will "keep your sunny side up" far into the dinner hour.

How to get there: 136 Malaga Street, St. Augustine. Open for breakfast and lunch only. Take Interstate 95 to U.S. 1 into St. Augustine. U.S. 1 becomes Ponce De Leon Blvd. when it curves north at the city limits. At the curve, turn right onto Malaga Street. Malaga Street Depot, next to the bus depot, is in the middle of the block.

While you're here: Many books have been written on what to do while in St. Augustine. As the oldest city in the United States, it is filled with history. The Restoration Area, just six blocks from Malaga Street, is a fascinating, authentic journey into the past. No cars are allowed in the area. If you have bicycles, bring them. It is the best way to tour the city. You can also take a Sightseeing Train or one of the many horse-drawn carriages which include informative narration. Be sure to visit Castillo de San Marcos, a huge fortress made completely of native coquina shells and surrounded by a moat. It was begun in 1672 and completed several years later.

St. Augustine is one place in Florida that you can visit in the spring without competing with huge crowds. Summer is the busiest season — the St. Augustine Fourth of July celebration shouldn't be missed.

MALAGA STREET DEPOT
ST. AUGUSTINE

GAZPACHO SOUP

2	28 oz. cans pear-shaped tomatoes
2	cucumbers (peeled, diced)
2	green peppers (diced)
1	medium onion (chopped, large chunks)
1	clove garlic
¼	c. olive oil
2	T. red wine vingar
2	t. fresh thyme
2	t. fresh oregano
2	t. fresh Cilantro (Chinese parsley — may substitute fresh parsley if not available)
2	t. fresh parsley
2	t. ground cumin
	salt and pepper to taste
	Jalapeno peppers (optional)
	garlic croutons
	scallions (sliced)

1. Crush tomatoes with hand in large bowl.
2. Add all other ingredients except croutons and scallions.
3. Chill. Dish into bowls and garnish with croutons and scallions.

Serves: 4
Preparation: 20 minutes
Chill: 2-3 hours

"If at all possible, use fresh herbs as it is more flavorful!"

— NOTES —

PESTO SAUCE

½   c. fresh parsley (chopped fine)
½   c. fresh basil (chopped fine)
½   c. Parmesan cheese (grated fresh)
1   T. lemon juice
2   t. fresh garlic (minced)
½-¾ c. olive oil
    salt and pepper to taste

1. Mix parsley, basil, Parmesan cheese, lemon juice, and garlic together.
2. Add olive oil until mixture is the thickness of ketchup.
3. Add salt and pepper. Keep on hand for seasoning. The longer sauce sits the better it tastes.

*NOTE: Will last in refrigerator for several months, so make up a batch!

"Adds a great taste to vegetables. We especially like it combined with fresh broccoli."

— NOTES —

BREAKFAST TACOS

2	eggs (beaten)
¼	c. green peppers (diced)
¼	c. onions (diced)
1	corn tortilla
3	T. refried beans
⅓	c. cheddar cheese (shredded)
	picante sauce

— PICANTE SAUCE —

1	green pepper (diced)
1	small onion (diced)
3-4	Jalapeno peppers (minced)
1	clove garlic (crushed)
28	oz. can pear-shaped tomatoes (crushed with hand)
1	T. + 1 t. cider vinegar
2	t. oregano
1	bay leaf
	dash ground cumin
1	T. + 1 t. fresh Cilantro (may substitute fresh parsley)
	juice of one lemon

— PICANTE SAUCE —

1. Mix all ingredients for sauce together.

— TACOS —

2. Combine eggs, green pepper, and onions on griddle or in saute pan. Cook.
3. Heat corn tortilla briefly on griddle.
4. Place tortilla on plate. Top with eggs and refried beans. Fold in sides to seal.
5. Top with cheese and liberal amount of picante sauce.
6. Place under broiler for few seconds.

NOTE: The picante sauce can be kept in the refrigerator for future use. You will find many uses for it (great for dipping tortilla chips).

Serves: 1
Preparation: 15 minutes for sauce/5 minutes for tacos
Cooking: 5 minutes

"A most unusual breakfast dish!"

— NOTES —

BROCCOLI TOSKA
("Inside Out Omelet")

8-10 4"spears fresh broccoli (can use ¾ pkg. frozen)
½ c. water
4 eggs
2-2½ T. pesto sauce (See recipe on page 191)
2 t. Parmesan cheese
½ c. flour
2 T. olive oil
2 T. butter
fresh garlic (crushed)
½ lemon
⅓ c. sherry
1½ T. flour
⅓ c. broccoli broth (saved from cooking broccoli)
3 oz. (1 c.) Swiss cheese (shredded)
Optional: 1 c. hollandaise sauce (pkg. mix makes 1 c. —
follow directions)

1. Cook broccoli al dente in shallow pan in ½ cup water. Remove broccoli and save broth.
2. In small bowl mix eggs, pesto sauce, and Parmesan cheese.
3. Lightly flour broccoli spears. Drop into egg batter bowl.
4. In a 9" or 10" skillet or saute pan (best with non-stick surface) heat olive oil and butter.
5. Pour broccoli and egg batter into skillet. Cook until quite brown on outside edge.
6. Carefully turn over and sprinkle touch of garlic on top. Next, add juice of lemon and sherry. Sprinkle flour into liquids around edges of pan.
7. Add broccoli broth. Shake pan to get liquid to thicken a little around edges of egg.
8. Place Swiss cheese over top. Slide under broiler briefly to melt cheese and brown.
9. Cut and place on plates. Salt and pepper. Top with hollandaise sauce, if desired.

Serves: 2-6 (depending on if it is to be entree or
      side dish)
Preparation: 30 minutes
Cooking: 30 minutes

"Bon Appetit! Most unusual but yummy!"

— NOTES —

— NOTES —

Cafe Anastasia

— St. Augustine —

Though Cafe Anastasia is slightly higher in price than other "underground gourmet" establishments selected for this book, it came highly recommended and proved to be very special in both cuisine and management.

The Cafe, located on Anastasia Island in St. Augustine, is a reflection of its owners Patty Johnson and Francoise Soubrane.

The restaurant, seating just 30 people, is comfortably simple. A black and white checkerboard pattern floor determines the decor, which is carried out by dark mahogany chairs and tables covered by white linen cloths. An antique piano is the only accessory. Gaily colored parrots provide the focal points of color...on one side of the restaurant printed on a huge wall hanging, and a stuffed version perched above the tables on the other side.

Patty and Francoise bought the restaurant in 1980. Francoise, born and raised in Paris, provides a French influence to both the cuisine and the atmosphere. Patty, who calls herself "Julia's child," came to St. Augustine from Mobile, Alabama. Both had been regulars in the restaurant, previously called the

Ragwood Cafe. When it came up for sale, they grabbed it.

Vegetarians will enjoy the Anastasia Omelet, an omelet made with mushrooms, sherry, scallions and Swiss cheese. Chicken lovers may select the menu favorite Chicken with Peppercorn Sauce, a lightly battered fillet that is sauteed and garnished with a heavenly, creamy peppercorn sauce. Got a yen for Oriental cuisine? The Panfried Japanese Noodle dish is a delicious medley of quickly sauteed vegetables with buckwheat noodles, seasoned with garlic. (Bring some mints.) Fish Meuniere, Shrimp Sauce Moutarde and Fish Banana Curry (the latter two are not always on the menu) are designed for seafood lovers (there are *more* of them in St. Augustine).

Yes, you beef lovers, there is something in this for you, too. The Tournedos Parisienne is very tender beef fillets, cooked to your liking, topped with fresh mushrooms, onion, and Francoise and Patty's perfected Bearnaise sauce. In addition, Patty's quiche of the day, a specialty that she hopes will some day be packaged by Stouffer's, is always on the chalkboard.

Appetizers include the extraordinary Oysters Giovanni, broiled with lemon, butter, cognac and seasoned stuffing. Prepare this recipe at home and your raw-oyster-loving friends will never go raw again!

A soup of the day varies with the season. Summer soups are always cold, such as "lemon grass" and cucumber soups. Winter soups are served hot. (Hope that their authentic French Onion soup is being served on your visit. It is loaded with baby round Swiss cheese, broiled until the cheese bubbles and is lightly browned. A dash of cognac and lavender perk up the flavor.)

Desserts are rich and loaded with calories, as one would expect from a Parisienne. Top off your meal with one of the house coffees, such as Expresso, Cappuccino or Cafe Brulot Flambe, made with cognac, clove and cinnamon.

Be prepared to wait — with just one cook and one stove, it's inevitable. But then, anything worth having is worth waiting for.

Also, since the restaurant is available any night of the week for private groups, don't be surprised to find a sign in the window that it's closed that night. And be patient if you go late in the afternoon and find a "Gone Fishing" sign — they'll be right back. They are so adamant that their seafood be as fresh as possible that they don't even own a freezer. So, many days require two trips down to the docks to select fish, shrimp and oysters.

A chalkboard on the back wall carries a message with words from a song Francoise often sings to customers — "Chacun fait ce qui lui plait!" meaning, "Everyone do as you please!"

How to get there: *415 Anastasia Boulevard, St. Augustine. From U.S. 1 South, take the Bridge of Lions on King Street across to Anastasia Island. Cafe Anastasia is on your right. If you come to the Alligator Farm or the lighthouse, you've gone too far. Cafe Anastasia is open Wednesday through Saturday.*

While you're here: *You're just a few blocks from one of the most beautiful beaches in Florida, far less developed than those south of St. Augustine (such as Daytona Beach). You'll enjoy the relative amount of privacy. Cars are allowed to drive along the beach, but if you go at night, you'll have a fabulous, serene walk under a star-filled sky. There are few hotels, and dramatic differences in tides force construction far away from the water line. Be sure to visit Capt. Jim's Conch House for a beautiful waterside view just around the corner.*

CAFE ANASTASIA
ST. AUGUSTINE

OYSTERS GIOVANNI

2	c. crushed Ritz crackers (approx. 45 crackers)
¾	c. scallions (chopped)
2	t. garlic (minced)
½	c. fresh parsley (chopped)
2	t. dillweed
1	pt. oysters (drained well)
30	oyster shells or 6 ramekins
3	lemons
	cognac
½	c. clarified butter

1. Mix crackers, scallions, garlic, parsley and dillweed together.
2. Place well drained oysters in shells or ramekins.
3. Squeeze lemons over oysters and add a few drops of cognac to each shell.
4. Cover generously with cracker mixture and pour butter on top of all.
5. Place under broiler (rack should be in second position from the top).
6. Cook until golden brown, about 3-5 minutes.

Serves: 5-6 as appetizer
Preparation: 10 minutes
Cooking: 5 minutes

"An oyster lover's delight!"

— NOTES —

SHRIMP MOUTARDE

2	T. butter
2	T. scallions (chopped)
1	t. garlic (chopped)
1	T. lemon juice
1	T. Dijon mustard
½	c. dry white wine (use good brand)
½	c. whipping cream
1	lb. medium-large shrimp (shelled and cleaned)

1. In large pan over high heat, saute scallions and garlic in butter.
2. Add lemon juice, mustard, and white wine. Reduce 15 seconds.
3. Add cream. Bring to boil.
4. Add shrimp (don't crowd!). Cook for 2-3 minutes. Remove with slotted spoon. Cook remaining shrimp.
5. Continue stirring sauce until it thickens. Pour sauce over shrimp.

Serves: 4
Preparation: 15 minutes
Cooking: 10 minutes

"An easy but elegant dish. Serve over rice and with a pretty green vegetable!"

— NOTES —

FISH BANANA CURRY

4	fillets, medium thickness (Red Snapper preferred)
1	egg (beaten)
½	c. milk
2	bananas (cut in half and sliced down middle)
	curry powder
¼	c. flour
1	T. Crisco oil
1	T. olive oil
4	T. butter
1	lemon
	sherry
¼	c. fresh parsley (chopped)

1. Place fillets in mixture of egg and milk. Remove. Place on dinner plate. Prepare bananas and place along sides.
2. Generously sprinkle curry powder over fish and bananas. Lightly flour.
3. In large saute pan, over high heat, heat oils and 1 T. butter. Place bananas, flat side down in pan. Saute until golden brown.
4. Turn bananas over. Sprinkle lemon juice and sherry on each. Transfer to dinner plates.
5. Add fillets to pan, skin side up. Cook for few minutes. Turn over and sprinkle lemon and sherry on each. Transfer to plates.
6. In small pan heat 3 T. butter, parsley, and lemon juice. Pour over fillets on dinner plates.

Serves: 4
Preparation: 10 minutes
Cooking: 5 minutes

"The curry taste is delicious with Snapper. Chutney is a nice complement."

CHOCOLATE MOUSSE

5	1-oz. squares unsweetened chocolate
1	T. butter
¼	t. vanilla extract
1	large orange
1	c. sugar
6	eggs
	whipped cream
	Cointreau

1. Break up chocolate. Melt slowly in double boiler with butter and vanilla.
2. Meanwhile, squeeze orange and add juice to sugar in a small saucepan. Heat until sugar is dissolved, stirring occasionally.
3. Separate eggs, placing whites in refrigerator.
4. In large mixing bowl, beat egg yolks while slowly adding in the syrup. Continue beating until thick and lightly colored (10-20 minutes).
5. Fold melted chocolate into egg yolk mixture.
6. Beat egg whites until stiff peaks form. Gently and carefully fold one-quarter of the egg whites into the chocolate mixture. Fold in the remaining three-quarters.
7. Carefully place mousse into individual dessert dishes. Chill 3-5 hours. Top with whipped cream and Cointreau.

Serves: 8
Preparation: 30 minutes
Cooking: 15 minutes
Chill: 3-5 hours

"A rich dessert with a lovely hint of orange!"

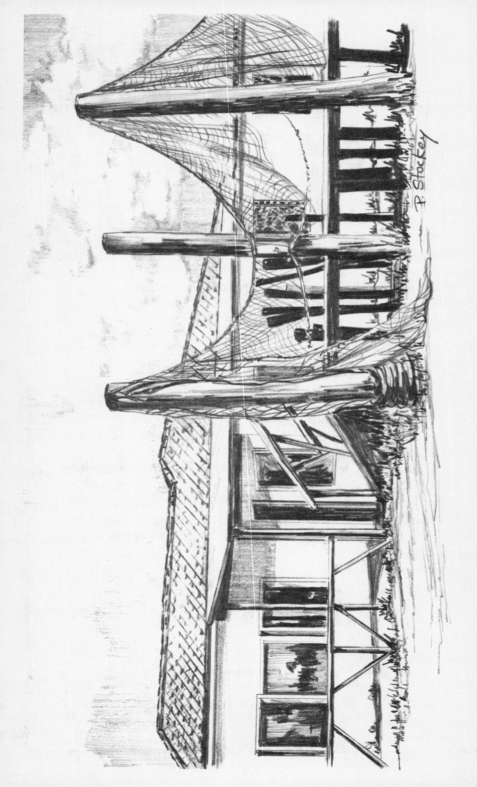

The Village Sunken Shack(?) ... Brad Gist(?)

P. Stockey

The Vilano Seafood Shack

...his pride in his occupation, surpasses the pride of kings.
— Mark Twain, 1883

— Vilano Beach —

Three St. Augustine restaurants are featured in this book, an easily justified disproportionate focus since there are 190 restaurants in this charming city of just 15,000 residents. That's one restaurant for every fifteen families! Of course, they share them — with thousands of visitors each year, primarily during the summer months.

St. Augustine is the oldest city in the United States. Often called the City of the Centuries, because of its antiquity, it was discovered by the Spanish explorer Don Juan Ponce de Leon in 1513, 55 years before the Pilgrims landed at Plymouth Rock. It was named for the saint whose feast day was celebrated the day of landing.

Though four flags have flown over the city — Spanish, British, Confederate, and American — the area has preserved its Spanish roots and restored much of its 18th-century construction. What has happened in between is a fascinating story of love, war and honor, too long a story to recite here, but one you will discover as a living legend when you visit this city.

The Vilano Seafood Shack, on Vilano Beach, is just a mile north and east of the St. Augustine city limits. At 8:00 on a weeknight, the parking area around the casual beach hut is full, one of the best signs of a book-worthy restaurant.

Owners Cynthia and Nathan Vestal purchased the "Shack," actually more a cottage in design and atmosphere, in November of 1980. The building was built in the late 1920s to be used as a service station, but was shortly thereafter converted to a restaurant. It reflects the atmosphere of this quiet, rustic beach community in its decor with picnic tables, wood-slat walls, beamed ceilings and natural air conditioning...the type of decor that is accidentally charming, rather than designed to be so.

But the exceptional quality of food served in the seaside eatery is no accident. It is the result of years of intense study and dedication to the art of food preparation.

Nathan has spent many years in the gourmet restaurant business, many of those years with French chefs. Unlike many cooks, he views his position not as a job, but as a profession of which he is impressively proud.

Nathan is a master of sauteing and broiling methods of seafood preparation, but if you insist on deep-fried, try the grouper fillet and work your way from a teaspoon of tartar sauce with each bite to actually scraping off the light batter to appreciate fully the intrinsic value of the grouper flavor. Nathan selects the fish from the docks the day it's served and bathes it in a delicious garlic marinade before blanketing in batter.

All of Nathan's fish and seafood (99% of the menu) get this personal attention. Each day he travels from Mayport to Ponce Inlet in search of the best catches. Cynthia's and Nathan's philosophy about fish freshness is, "Lose a day's time, lose business." It makes an ocean of difference.

Aside from the Catch of the Day, often snapper or grouper, the menu offers oysters, scallops, shrimp and clams — broiled, sauteed or deep-fried. Blue crabs are served when available. Additional specialties include Minorcan clam chowder or oyster stew, conch fritters, sauteed mushrooms, potato skins with cheese, or stuffed mushrooms.

We saved the best for last. The crab meat stuffed mushrooms may prompt an immediate vocal reaction — they are fabulous. The secret is in the fresh crab meat (many other places use canned), the amount, Datil peppers (a Minorcan staple), and all the extras Nathan throws in. The same recipe is used in the stuffed shrimp and stuffed catch of the day.

The Minorcan heritage of St. Augustine is alive and well at the Seafood Shack. The Minorcans, early settlers of the area from the Mediterranean island of Minorca, are responsible for many of today's customs and recipes used in the city's restaurants. The Datil pepper is a key ingredient in Minorcan food. It does wonders for the Seafood Shack's clam chowder, crab meat stuffing and conch fritters.

One of the many special extras provided by Cynthia and Nathan is that if you request, and they have all the ingredients, they will prepare anything your way. They say several of their favorite recipes were "discovered" through customers' special requests, including the Sauteed Fish recipe.

The menu's claim, "You can get fresh with us," is more than a cute play on words...fresh *is* the Vilano Seafood Shack in a word. But, to embellish, it is also a seaside shanty that fishes for compliments...and catches them by the schoolful.

How to get there: Take A1A to Vilano Beach, 1½ miles northeast of St. Augustine, one-half mile east of the Vilano Beach bridge. The Seafood Shack is on the corner of the 90° turn on A1A. Closed Tuesday.

While you're here: Anastasia Island State Recreation Area, on A1A South across from the Matanzas River is a perfect location for enjoying St. Augustine and its beaches. It is from a large lagoon here that Spaniards quarried rocks from the original coquina vein to build many of the historical structures, still intact in the city's restoration area. It's within bicycle distance (if you are semi-in shape) of most of the places you'll want to see. Also, if you visit in June, July or August, don't miss **The Cross and the Sword***, a fascinating play based on St. Augustine's history, performed in the St. Augustine Ampitheatre.*

THE VILANO SEAFOOD SHACK
VILANO BEACH

THE SHACK'S STUFFED MUSHROOMS

1	lb. fresh mushrooms (largest you can find)
2	slices whole wheat bread
4	T. butter
¼	c. celery (minced)
¼	c. onions (minced)
¼	t. oregano
⅛	t. thyme
1¼	t. Worcestershire sauce
⅛	t. salt
¼	t. pepper
2	dashes tabasco sauce
1	c. crab meat (frozen or canned)
	paprika
	lemon wedges (garnish)
⅛	of a Datil pepper (minced)
	(may substitute very hot peppers)

1. Remove stems from mushrooms. Place caps in shallow baking dish.
2. Remove crusts from bread. Crumble remaining bread in bowl. In small skillet place 2 T. butter and saute celery and onions until tender. Add to bowl with bread.
4. Add all spices, 2 T. melted butter, and crab meat. Mix well.
5. Stuff mushrooms, mounding well using all stuffing. Sprinkle with paprika.
6. Bake in 350°F oven for 12-15 minutes. Garnish with lemon wedges.

Makes: 8-12
Preparation: 15 minutes
Cooking: 15 minutes

"Great for an appetizer or accompaniment to a fine meal."

NATHAN'S SAUTEED SNAPPER VILANO

½   c. butter
4   snapper fillets (or any white fish fillets)
    flour for dusting
½   lemon
1   t. sherry (use a good brand)
1   T. capers

1. Heat butter in skillet until it just begins to boil.
3. Cook each side 3-5 minutes, depending on thickness.
4. When cooked on both sides, squeeze lemon over fillets and add sherry and capers.
5. Allow edges of fish to crispen. Serve by spooning capers over fillets.

Serves: 4
Preparation: 5 minutes
Cooking: 5 minutes

"The sherry and capers add the zing — easy!"

— NOTES —

CINDY'S FISH SPREAD

1   lb. fish (flaked) from large fish carcasses OR
    1 lb. fresh fillets (2 c. — flaked and cooked)
1   c. sour cream
¼   c. onion (chopped)
2-3 dashes tabasco
1-2 dashes Worcestershire sauce
    lots of salt and pepper to taste
2-3 drops Liquid Smoke
    crackers

1. Flake fish fillets, or, if using fish from carcasses
    steam in basket over boiling water for 15 minutes
    until fish loosens from bones (the tastiest meat is
    out of the jawbones). Pick out meat.
2. Add sour cream to meat until spreading
    consistency.
3. Add remaining ingredients. Mix well.
4. Spread on wafer crackers. Escort brand is an
    excellent choice.
5. You may substitute crab meat for fish.

Serves: 12-15 as an appetizer
Preparation: 15 minutes

"The consistency is heavenly... an easy party dish."

Whitey's Fish Camp

Doubt not but angling will prove to be so pleasant, that it will prove to be, like virtue, a reward to itself.
— Izaak Walton, 17th century author

— Orange Park —

Whitey's Fish Camp, 15 miles southwest of Jacksonville in Orange Park, is a true Florida fish camp. Not only is it famous for fresh-water fish and smoked pork and chicken, it is a popular spot for locals to gather and exchange news of the community and, of course, incredible fish stories.

The numbers served at Whitey's Fish Camp are testimony to the quality of Florida home cooking. Approximately 7,000 are served each week, consuming over a ton of catfish, Whitey's specialty. The national acclaim achieved through the recommendations of well-traveled celebrities such as golf pro Lee Trevino (one of the camp's regulars), the late John Belushi, and musical entertainment stars such as Three Dog Night are also testimony to the exceptional food and atmosphere.

Whitey and Ann Ham, owners of Whitey's Fish Camp for 20 years, started with nine barstools, a sandwich menu, draft beer, and a pool table. The restaurant's popularity grew, as did the building. The additions give the restaurant an interesting exterior profile. Though 140 customers can now be accommodated, there isn't enough room to avoid long lines on the weekends. Weather permitting, outside picnic tables make room for more.

The entire Ham family is now involved in running the Fish Camp. Ann and Whitey's son runs the restaurant when they are on the road. Ann is active in Bass 'n' Gals, a national organization of 15,000 women who compete in a circuit of bass fishing tournaments across the country. Approximately 150 women compete regularly in the eight competitions held annually. In addition to these, she competes on a local level at least once a month. And, despite continually competing, Ann is fishing around the local waters of the St. John's River whenever she can.

Whitey has given up competition fishing in favor of supporting his wife, but is considered the local expert of "hot spots" in the proximity of his camp. Every bit as popular as the restaurant is his bait shop and fishing boat rental service, which include his expert advice on bringing home a praiseworthy catch.

The restaurant, which sits off the road in a serene setting of Spanish moss-covered trees on a feeder creek of the St. John's River at Doctor's Lake, is as "real Florida" on the exterior as it is inside. The only element that separates them is the contrast between the peaceful isolation of the exterior, and the bustle of activity inside at all hours of the day and night.

The walls are filled with prize-catch fish, 52 of which are bass, Florida's state fresh-water fish. According to Whitey, his restaurant displays the largest bass ever mounted, a whopping 18-pounder. The largest ever recorded catch was a 22-pounder.

The decor is pure sportsman, as well as the atmosphere. At 2:00 on a Wednesday afternoon, the joviality was more the level of a weekend evening at most other community gathering spots. Outside, a dozen men had gathered for an impromptu guitar-accompanied sing-along.

The clientele is primarily local, though very popular with Jacksonville professionals who have only a 15 to 30-minute drive to escape the city to this oasis of rustic, natural beauty enhanced by great eating. Two nearby naval stations account for a good number of customers. Often, on weekends, Jacksonville yacht clubs will organize outings for their members to Whitey's Fish Camp, which is easily reached via the St. John's River. The large and expensive sailing yachts (as well as their owners) provide an interesting contrast to the Camp's rustic simplicity. But, good food knows no boundaries of class echelons.

The menu is as varied as the clientele. Frog Legs, Alligator, Turtle, Catfish and Quail are featured dinners. The Catfish Dinner, the most popular, is an all-you-can-eat affair seven days a week. Though more than 20 of the menu choices are fresh fish and seafood entrees, Whitey's Fish Camp is also well-known for its barbecue.

About the only complaint ever heard at Whitey's Fish Camp concerns the size of the catfish being served that day. Catfish vary greatly in taste according to size, and everyone has a different idea of what size is best.

Whatever the size, no one does it better than Whitey's Fish Camp. When it comes to a novel eatery, Whitey's Fish Camp is quite a fish story!

How to get there: *It's easier to get there than it sounds. Take U.S. 301 to County Road 218 east into Middleburg. Then take S.R. 21 north out of town to County Road 220. Head east again and when you cross the second bridge, you will see Whitey's Fish Camp on your left.*

While you're here: *Talk to Whitey about taking a professionally guided bass search on his 17-foot, fully equipped bass boat. If they are out there, and they are, Whitey will find them. He knows them all by name!*

CATFISH CHOWDER

1½	lbs. fresh water catfish
2	quarts of water
¼	lb. salt pork (or bacon)
2	medium onions (chopped)
2	medium potatoes (diced)
1	T. Accent
	tabasco to taste
	salt and pepper to taste

1. Clean and wash catfish. Cook in 2 quarts water until fish starts to come away from bone (about 15-20 minutes).
2. Meanwhile fry salt pork until crisp. Chop and set aside with drippings.
3. Carefully remove fish from bones. Return boned fish, and all other ingredients to pot.
4. Bring back to boil and simmer until potatoes and onions are tender, about 10-15 minutes.

Makes: 2 quarts
Preparation: 15 minutes
Cooking: 30-40 minutes

"Make up a batch to put in the freezer! You'll love it!"

— NOTES —

SWEET 'N SOUR COLE SLAW

1   **small head green cabbage (shredded)**
2   **medium carrots (grated)**
1   **c. sugar**
1   **c. vinegar**
½   **c. water**
½   **c. salad oil**
1   **T. celery seed**
1   **T. Accent**
      salt and pepper to taste
      Optional: Purple cabbage and/or green pepper

1. Mix all above ingredients well.
2. Let stand for 1 hour before serving.

Serves: 4-5
Preparation: 20 minutes
Chill: 1 hour

"The name describes it all!"

— NOTES —

Beignets

— Jacksonville —

You might think you've been misled when you pull up to Beignets, located in a small commercial strip on University Boulevard West in Jacksonville. The sign over the door says "Beignets — French Doughnuts." No mention is made of full course dining.

But, once inside, the aroma of French Creole cooking (not quite as hot as Spanish Creole) will reassure you of the credibility of this recommendation.

Beignets, owned by sisters Lois Harrell and Pat Sheffield, is a quaint and unusual restaurant that serves just two main courses each day. One is Red Beans and Rice; the other varies from week to week.

Both Lois and Pat were born in New Orleans and spent a great deal of time in France while growing up. Raised on French Creole cooking, they know how it is prepared and how it should taste as well as the rest of us know hamburgers.

When the cafe was first opened, beignets were the single item offered from the kitchen. Lois had intended it to stay that way. But as delicious as the French doughnuts are (they are actually more like fritters), sales were not enough to justify the rent. They decided to add lunch and dinner, just one dish each day, but always a home-cooked French Creole dish, perfectly prepared.

Lois would make enough for about 25 dinners. That's all they wanted to serve. There was no fanfare, no advertising, not even a mention of lunches or dinners on the sign out front. There still isn't.

"The Lord must be watching over me. Because despite my never considering myself a kitchen gourmet, the restaurant has become very popular," Lois says.

Her only desire was to bring New Orleans' popular beignets to the Jacksonville area. They had been her favorite food growing up and she knew others would develop the same love for these French treats. So, without a recipe to go by, relying on her taste buds alone, she began to experiment. Months went by before she knew she had just the right proportions and cooking time. Her desire for perfection was worth the effort. Her beignets are delicious...light and airy on the inside; crisp, but not greasy, on the outside. The line for her beignets usually begins to form at 7 a.m.

Lois and Pat still operate on a very small scale, though. Lois prepares the dish of the day, which appears on a blackboard near the door, in the morning.

"When it's gone, we close," she says. "That usually happens around 6:00 or 7:00 in the evening."

Some of the dishes that are served, often by Lois herself, include Shrimp Creole, Redfish Court Bouillon (a fish stew), Chicken Creole, Crab and Shrimp Gumbos, and Chicken Jambalaya. The dishes are sometimes accompanied by homemade Creole soups, and always by a special french bread that is made only in Mobile, Alabama. Lois or Pat picks it up at the bus station two or three times a week. It has become so popular with restaurant regulars that it is now sold by the loaf for take-home use.

The coffee that many choose to accompany their beignets is also special. It is a hand-blended mixture of fresh-ground coffee beans and chicory, creating a rich and flavorful brew. It is brewed fresh every half hour, and may also be served with cream and a dab of sweet whipping cream...*vive la France!*

Like it or not, Lois, you can't keep food like this a secret for long!

How to get there: *Take Interstate 95 to University Boulevard West five miles south of the St. John's River. Head west about one and a half miles. Beignets is on the south side of the Boulevard, across from Albertson's.*

While you're here: *This area of Jacksonville offers some of the finest house-gazing anywhere. If you're from any part of the State south of Orlando and like to reminisce about the neighborhoods common to the northern state you once called home, you can do it here. Try a drive along San Jose Boulevard. And, if you can live with a spell of envy, see how the exceptionally wealthy live out on Ponte Vedra Beach. Several of the homes have been featured in centerfolds of national magazines. If you continue down A1A, near South Ponte Vedra Beach, you can find long stretches of completely undeveloped beach with public access.*

RED BEANS
(Allow To Soak Overnight)

1   lb. dry kidney beans (red beans)
2   large onions (chopped)
2   cloves garlic (minced)
1   bay leaf
¼   t. cumin powder
1   t. parsley
    dash or two of hot pepper sauce
1   T. sugar
    salt and pepper to taste
    dash Worcestershire sauce
1   lb. sausage and/or diced ham

1. Soak beans overnight in 4 c. water in large saucepan. Rinse several times. Cover well with water.
2. Add onions, garlic, and bay leaf. Simmer for at least 2 hours or until beans are tender and soft.
3. Add remaining ingredients and cook for ½ hour more. Serve over rice or with buttery tasting crackers along side.

Serves: 4
Preparation: overnight soaking/10 minutes
Cooking: 3 hours

"On cold chilly nights, a great body warmer!"

— NOTES —

SHRIMP CREOLE

2	lbs. medium shrimp (in shells)
2¼	c. water
2	T. butter
2	T. flour
½	large onion (diced)
1	green pepper (diced)
2	cloves garlic (minced)
½	c. tomato paste
2	T. fresh parsley (minced)
3-4	scallions (cut crosswise)
	salt and pepper to taste

1. Shell and clean shrimp. Place shells in water and cook to make stock. Put shrimp aside.
2. In large skillet, brown butter, add flour and stir to make paste.
3. Brown onions, green pepper, and garlic in skillet with paste.
4. Drain stock from shells and add 2 c. of stock to skillet along with tomato paste. Cook for 1 hour or until thick.
5. Add shrimp, parsley, scallions, salt and pepper.
6. Cook until shrimp are tender. Do not overcook. Serve over rice.

Serves: 6
Preparation: 15 minutes
Cooking: 1½ hours

"A colorful dish with a taste to match!"

— NOTES —

CHICKEN JAMBALAYA

3	T. butter
3	T. flour
2	large onions (chopped)
1	bunch scallions (chopped)
1	red pepper (chopped)
2	T. parsley (fresh best)
¼	t. basil
	salt and pepper
	several dashes hot sauce
3	c. water
3	chicken bouillon cubes
2	lbs. cooked white chicken (cubed-about 3-4 c.)

1. Brown butter in large skillet. Stir in flour and blend to make paste.
2. Add vegetables and brown. Add spices, seasonings, water, and bouillon cubes. Simmer for 1 hour.
3. Add chicken and thicken with equal amounts of butter and flour if necessary. Heat through.
4. Serve over white rice, dirty rice, or mixed white and wild rice.

Serves: 4
Preparation: 10 minutes
Cooking: 1 hour 10 minutes

"The red pepper adds a delightful color to a most enchanting dish!"

— NOTES —

— NOTES —

Hopkins Boarding House, Pensacola, Florida

Hopkins Boarding House

— Pensacola —

Pensacola is second only to St. Augustine in being the oldest city in the United States. Its 400 years of history are evident in its architecture, people and traditions. More so than any other city in this "underground gourmet" tour, Pensacola has kept its traditions alive through active restoration programs, city festivals and celebrations and the strong will of the residents.

In the heart of the North Hill preservation area is a turn-of-the-century Victorian-style home that is keeping alive a dining tradition that may well not exist anywhere else in the state.

Hopkins Boarding House is celebrated locally and beyond for down-home cooking served family style.

You begin your journey into the past as you walk up the tree-shaded walkway with only a simple sign to tell you that you're entering the right house.

Pull up a rocking chair on the breezy front porch and wait for your name to be called in to supper. While overlooking the quiet oak-shaded streets, listen to locals catching up on neighborhood news, hashing over current events and talking about the weather, just like the "old days."

Once inside, you're greeted by Arkie Bell Hopkins, affectionately called Ma Hopkins, who graciously takes you into her home. Carved wooden fireplaces, high ceilings, antique furniture, plate rails, and family mementos and portraits, along with the dining atmosphere itself, give the boarding house the feel of a Norman Rockwell painting.

You'll be seated in one of three small dining rooms with a total of just six large tables. If you don't like the idea of sitting with people you've never met, you'll have to bring your own crowd. But you'll be missing out on half the fun of eating here.

The food and fixin's are already on the table when you sit down. Southern fried chicken, rice and gravy, sliced carrots, okra and stewed tomatoes, black-eyed peas, potato salad, yellow squash casserole, sliced tomatoes, cottage cheese, hot corn muffins, bread and butter, and banana pudding are passed around the table. Take all you want, and when you want more just ask someone to pass it. That's how you get the conversation going. The bowls are kept filled and freshened until you're stuffed. Your milk or iced tea glass is also kept filled by the good-natured waitresses.

Don't be insulted if your table company leaves you halfway through your meal. Everyone at the table comes and goes as they please, with quick changes of fresh table settings in between. When you're through, it is customary to take your own plate to the kitchen. If you came from a large family this will all make you feel quite at home. On your way out you pay for your meal — the same low price as everyone else.

Fried chicken is the featured dish three days a week. Chicken and dumplings, beef stew, roast beef, and ham and liver are served on the alternating days. Vegetables change from season to season and day to day, but they are always fresh and prepared without the "magic" of microwaves or food processors. Even the beans are fresh from the garden and hand-snapped, all four bushels each day.

Ma Hopkins runs her "roost" with a firm but loving hand. No smoking is allowed in the house and if anyone gets out of hand, or takes unwelcome advantage of the "all-you-can-eat" arrangement, she "calls them down."

Ma conceived the idea of opening a boarding house 38 years ago. Her first location quickly outgrew itself. In 1951 she moved to the present location where she rents out five rooms upstairs and feeds as many as a thousand a day. Though she admits she'd had no previous experience in running a restaurant, she had grown up on a farm nearby and well learned how to feed a large family off the land.

Ma Hopkins is considered as much an institution in this town as her boarding house. Like your favorite relative inviting the flock of "kinfolk" over to dinner, she greets, hugs, cheek-tweaks, bubbles for her favorites and scolds those who haven't come by for awhile. She supervises the excitement.

If you like the atmosphere of a large family Thanksgiving gathering, the friendly faces, continuous chattering, the very best of everyone's recipes contributing to the meal, and eating more of everything than you should (but not regretting a single bite), then Ma Hopkins would love to have you — nearly as much as you will love being there.

How to get there: 900 North Spring Street. Take Interstate 10 and U.S. 98 into downtown Pensacola. Take Palafox Highway to Cervantes Street. Turn west to Spring Street and north to address. Open for breakfast, lunch and dinner except Sunday evening and all day Monday.

While you're here: History is the focus of Pensacola attractions. Several museums including the Wentworth Museum and the Naval Aviation Museum are filled with interesting exhibits, and the free admission makes them excellent family activities. Take a walking tour of the Pensacola Historical District, around Seville Square and near the Hopkins Boarding House, by following a marked trail. You should also visit Fort Pickens on the tip of Santa Rosa Island, part of the Gulf Island National Seashore that is famous for its dune-filled, brilliant-white beaches.

FRIED SQUASH

2 lbs. yellow squash (may substitute zucchini)
salt
self-rising flour
fat for deep fat frying

1. Wash and slice squash into 1″ pieces.
2. Sprinkle salt over squash so that all pieces are lightly salted. (The salt draws out the extra liquid.)
3. Let sit 1 hour. Pour off liquid.
4. Dip and completely cover each piece in self-rising flour.
5. Fry in deep fat at 350°F until brown and crisp.

Serves: 6
Preparation: 1 hour 15 minutes
Cooking: 10 minutes

"A nice change for an old favorite!"

— NOTES —

SWEET POTATO SOUFFLE

4   **c. mashed sweet potatoes (if potatoes are dry,
add up to ½ c. evaporated milk)**
½   **c. sugar**
½   **c. butter or oleo**
½   **c. coconut**
⅓   **c. raisins**
1   **t. lemon extract or orange peel
miniature marshmallows**

1. While potatoes are hot, add all other ingredients.
2. Place in casserole dish. Cover with marshmallows.
3. Bake in 300 °F oven until marshmallows are brown,
   20-30 minutes.

Serves: 6
Preparation: 10 minutes
Cooking: 30 minutes

*"A nice accompaniment with smoked ham and perky
green vegetables!"*

— NOTES —

CHICKEN NOODLE CASSEROLE

1	**stewing chicken**
8	**oz. pkg. flat egg noodles**
16	**oz. can tomato sauce**
8	**oz. can tomato paste**
2	**onions (chopped)**
1	**green pepper (chopped)**
½	**c. celery (chopped)**
2	**t. oregano**
	salt and pepper to taste

1. Place stewing chicken in large pot. Cover with water and simmer until tender.
2. Remove chicken from broth and let cool. Set aside.
3. Cook noodles in broth until almost tender. Add remaining ingredients, cover, and simmer until vegetables are tender.
4. While vegetables are cooking, remove bones from chicken and return chicken to pot just before vegetables are done.

Serves: 6
Preparation: 30 minutes
Cooking: 1½ hours

"An inexpensive meal that rates a 10!"

— NOTES —

SQUASH CASSEROLE

3	lbs. summer squash (use small size)
¼	c. water
1	t. salt
½	c. onion (chopped)
½	c. butter
2	eggs (beaten)
¾	c. crushed Saltines
	salt and pepper to taste

1. Wash and trim squash. Cook in saucepan with water and salt until tender. Drain and mash.
2. Saute onion in butter until tender. Add to squash. Add eggs, Saltines, salt, and pepper. Mix and put in buttered casserole dish.
3. Bake in 325°F oven for 20 minutes.

Serves: 6
Preparation: 10 minutes
Cooking: 30 minutes

"The small, young squash have the best flavor!"

— NOTES —

BROCCOLI CASSEROLE

10	oz. pkg. frozen broccoli (chopped)
1	stalk celery (diced)
1	onion (diced)
½	c. butter or margarine
1	c. cooked rice
1	c. cheddar cheese (shredded)
1	c. cream of mushroom soup
	salt and pepper to taste

1. Cook broccoli in small amount of water until done. Drain.
2. Saute celery, and onion in butter.
3. Mix remaining ingredients in casserole dish. Bake in 350°F oven until bubbly, about 30 minutes.

Serves: 6
Preparation: 5 minutes
Cooking: 35 minutes

"An easy vegetable casserole that can be prepared the night before and baked just before serving!"

— NOTES —

Canary Cottage Restaurant

— Panama City —

Hedged between two modern buildings in the center of a busy commercial district on Harrison Avenue in Panama City is a tiny old cottage that is as befitting to its surroundings as a palm tree in New York. But like the mouse that roared, this unpretentious 100-year-old home is one of the area's best providers of plentiful home-cooked lunches, for a very small price.

The Canary Cottage, named for a canary-covered wallpaper that was discontinued after the cottage was named and the business licenses filed, is an international melting pot of gourmet cuisine.

Owner Dee Cambouris has had a variety of ethnic influences on her life. Husband Harry is Greek, her mother specialized in French cooking during her career as a chef, and her own interests, having been raised in the restaurant business, developed toward Italian and Spanish dishes, as well as exotic and complex desserts.

The result is a menu with courses from around the world. The sandwich list starts with German-style roast beef stacked on pumpernickel, with cucumbers, onion and a sauerbraten sauce. Choices also include a Greek steak sandwich on Greek bread with tomato sauce, peppers and onions; kosher-style corned beef and Swiss cheese; grilled crab meat and cheese; and an American-as-apple-pie roast beef sandwich. All are served with Greek potatoes, a zesty version of hash browns with onions, peppers, thyme, basil and oregano.

A lengthy and unusual salad list includes Wilted Spinach Delight, a spinach salad with tomatoes, scallions, bacon, mushrooms, cheese, hard-boiled egg and a spicy, warm dressing; Dee's Crab Delight on lettuce and spinach; Harry's Favorite, a compromise between a chef's and Greek salad; Chicken and Waldorf Salad combo plate; a Florida salad with marinated tomatoes, avocado, deviled eggs and cheeses; and a Grecian salad plate with tomatoes, peppers, onions, potatoes, feta cheese and marinated shrimp. Salads are served with finger sandwiches filled with a variety of spreads.

The most innovative salad concept is Dee's Trip Around the Kitchen. If you like to try everything, this one's for you. Dee does just that — a scoop of everything in the kitchen is attractively arranged on a plate with cold cuts, cheeses, deviled eggs, and finger sandwiches. It's a lot to handle, but priced no more than other items.

Dee's "trip" also includes a helping of the day's special, sometimes created by her mother, Tina Oelerich, who has a lifetime of gourmet cooking experience. There are two categories of specials, hot lunch and casserole. Casseroles have become a lost "art" in the restaurant industry, but a revival has begun. Though the casseroles vary daily, with new stars continually being discovered, they already include Pastichio, a layered Greek dish of chopped beef and tomato sauce, bread crumbs, macaroni, cheese and cream sauce; Moussaka; Chicken Tetrazzini; Ravioli Verdi, a shortcut to the luxury of Lasagna made with spinach and cream or spaghetti sauce; Spanakopeta, a pastry made with phyllo sheets, spinach, cheese and cream sauce; and Spanish Beef Casserole topped with cornbread.

You have to ask about desserts, because they are never the same. Dee loves to create extravagant desserts. She says her imagination is as free as an artist with his canvas. A recent hit was a Fruit Chantilly prepared in a meringue shell with a picturesque layer of garnish.

The Canary Cottage is actually the child of the Cambouris' first restaurant venture, Le Shack, now a popular gourmet dinner establishment in the city.

Dee, who was raised in Fort Lauderdale, and Harry were on vacation in this area in 1974, and were lured by the world's whitest beaches and recreational opportunities to make the visit permanent.

Harry found an old service station that he could envision as a hot dog "palace," on Dee's culinary condition that only the best kosher hot dogs would be served pan-fried with peppers, onions and potatoes in pita bread. Dee is the type of cook who would never serve anything "naked." The idea was a success and later, Pastichio and Moussaka were added to the menu.

They continued to add to the menu and decor and changed the name to Le Shack to reflect what had become an exclusive gourmet restaurant with an impressive wine list and clientele.

The Canary Cottage evolved from complaints that Le Shack was too far a drive from the retail hub of the city to be made on a lunch hour. So the Cambouris' found the cottage and after extensive interior remodeling and re-decorating, Dee's own work, it was opened for lunch and evening catering of weddings and parties. Decorated in flamingo, celery green and yellow, with high-back cane chairs, plants, cafe curtains, linen tablecloths and napkins, and old-fashioned china settings, the cottage is bright, cheerful and cozy, particularly for those fortunate to get a table on the enclosed sun porch.

If Dee could combine nationalities as well in world politics as she does on her menu, she might find herself at the United Nations some day!

How to get there: *803 Harrison Avenue, Panama City. Take Hwy. 231, the same as Harrison Avenue, into the city. The restaurant is three blocks south of Hardee's, across from the bank.*

While you're here: *Panama City's Ocean Opry features country music festivals every week, and every night during the summer. The Diver's Museum is just down the street from the restaurant, containing many of the unusual discoveries of the U.S. Naval diving teams. Panama City is also the gateway to what many claim to be the world's whitest beaches. Take U.S. 98 east or west for one of the most beautiful scenic drives in the state.*

WILTED SPINACH DELIGHT

½   lb. bacon
½-¾ c. sugar (or sugar substitute)
2   T. dry mustard
1   c. vinegar
¼   c. water
1   lb. fresh spinach (washed, cleaned, torn into
     bite-size pieces)
3   tomatoes (cut in wedges)
½   c. scallions (sliced)
2   hard boiled eggs (chopped fine)
½   c. sharp cheddar cheese
12   fresh mushrooms (sliced)

1. Place bacon in frying pan and fry until crisp.
   Remove bacon and allow to cool. Crumble.
   Set aside.
2. Add sugar, dry mustard, and vinegar to bacon
   drippings. Stir to blend. Add water. Stir. Bring to
   boil. Simmer 5 minutes while arranging salads.
3. Place spinach on salad plates. Arrange the other
   ingredients on top including the crumbled bacon.
4. Spoon the hot sauce over and serve immediately.

Variation: Use yellow squash which has been sliced
           thin.

Serves: 4-6
Preparation: 20 minutes
Cooking: 10 minutes

"A technicolor delight!"

— NOTES —

RAVIOLI VERDI

1	lb. frozen ravioli
½	c. butter (melted)
10	oz. pkg. fresh spinach (washed, stems removed)
4	oz. Romano cheese (grated)
½	lb. Ricotta cheese

— SAUCE —

2	T. butter
2	T. cornstarch
2	c. milk
¼	t. lemon extract
	salt and pepper to taste

— SAUCE —

1. In saucepan place butter and melt. Blend in cornstarch to a paste. Slowly add milk while stirring. Cook over low heat until thickened.
2. Add lemon extract, salt and pepper. Stir.

— ASSEMBLY —

3. Allow ravioli to defrost on their own.
4. Pour melted butter into bottom of 9x13" cake pan.
5. Place layer of ravioli (⅓) across bottom of pan. Follow with layer (⅓) of spinach. Sprinkle ⅓ of Romano cheese across spinach. Dot with ½ of Ricotta cheese. Add ½ of sauce.
6. Repeat layers another time.
7. Finish off with last of ravioli and spinach.
8. Sprinkle Romano cheese over all. Cover with aluminum foil.
9. Bake in 350°F oven for 1 hour.

   Variations: If you have leftover spaghetti sauce use instead of cream sauce. You can also use thin slices of ham.

Serves: 6-8
Preparation: 30 minutes
Cooking: 20 minutes/1 hour

"A most unusual but tasty lasagna-type dish!"

SPANISH CHOPPED BEEF CASSEROLE

2	lbs. ground round (can substitute ground chuck)
1	lb. ground sausage
1	green pepper (diced)
1	medium onion (diced)
2	carrots (diced)
3	stalks celery (diced)
16	oz. can tomato sauce
10	dashes tabasco sauce
	dash of granulated garlic
	salt and pepper to taste
15	oz. can red kidney beans, drained
15	oz. can whole kernel corn
½	c. water
½	c. shredded cheddar cheese
2	pkgs. corn muffin mix

1. In large fry pan brown meats. Add green pepper, onion, carrots, and celery. Cook until tender.
2. Add other ingredients except corn muffin mix. Stir and mix well.
3. Pour into large casserole.
4. Make corn muffin mix according to package directions. Pour over top of casserole.
5. Bake in 350°F oven for 30 minutes or until golden brown.

Serves: 8
Preparation: 20 minutes
Cooking: 45 minutes

"A whole delicious and colorful meal in a casserole!"

— NOTES —

KING'S CHOCOLATE

1   Duncan Hines Devil's Food Cake Mix
2   eggs
1½   c. water (minus 2 t.)
2   t. lemon extract
14   oz. dry chocolate frosting mix
2   c. boiling water
     whipped cream topping

1. Mix cake mix, eggs, water, and lemon extract in large bowl according to package directions.
2. Grease 9x13x2½ " baking dish. Pour in cake mix.
3. Sprinkle dry frosting mix over batter. **Very carefully,** pour the boiling water over the ingredients in the dish.
4. Bake in 350 °F oven for 30-40 minutes. Allow to cool until warm. Cut into squares. Place gently onto dessert plates. Top with whipped cream.

Makes: 9x11" cake
Preparation: 5 minutes
Cooking: 40 minutes

Variations: Use your imagination!
    Chocolate cake — rum extract — lemon frosting
    Cherry cake — rum extract — chocolate frosting
    Vanilla cake — brandy — vanilla frosting
    Orange cake — lemon extract — chocolate frosting

"An ancient Greek dish. It certainly must have been invented on Mt. Olympus!"

— NOTES —

— NOTES —

Spring Creek Restaurant

— Spring Creek —

Carolyn Lovel, owner of the Spring Creek Motel and Restaurant, 25 miles south of Tallahassee, speaks of her restaurant with as much love and pride as she would her first-born grandchild. And well she should.

The goal to locate backroads restaurants to include in this underground gourmet tour is well fulfilled here. Where Highway 365 ends, literally and rather abruptly with a half-foot drop into the sand, you will discover a very old and tiny fishing village with fewer than 100 residents, that takes advantage of the perfect combination of crystal-clear, spring-fed fresh water where it meets the Gulf of Mexico.

The proximity of the Spring Creek Restaurant to the fishermen's docks provides a menu of great variety and freshness, along with a scenic and quiet village atmosphere that is on Florida's endangered species list.

Carolyn and husband, Ben, purchased a nine-room motel and opened the restaurant in July, 1977. They had moved to Florida in 1939, living in several metropolitan areas before retreating to Spring Creek. Though Carolyn had no formal experience in the business, cooking is obviously a labor of love.

And, though comfortably gregarious, she prefers to stay in the kitchen.

The cottage-style restaurant is decorated with her own antique furniture. Hutches, bookcases, curio cabinets, porcelains, pottery and bric-a-brac lend a homey character to the 125-seat, sunny dining room. A large fireplace with full-wall stonework creates a ski lodge atmosphere, particularly during the cold North Florida winters. Her love of art is evident in several Florida scene paintings and prints.

The restaurant opens early in the morning to start the local fishermen out with hearty breakfasts. The mullet, eggs and grits breakfast is most popular.

The lunch and dinner menus feature a few typical seafood dishes such as lobster, boiled and fried shrimp, raw and fried oysters, catfish, grouper, flounder, scallops and speckled trout. For "landlubbers" there are steaks, fried chicken, chicken livers and gizzards, and pork chops.

There are also a number of atypical dishes such as broiled Shrimp Stuffed with Deviled Crab and wrapped in bacon, shark, stuffed soft-shell crabs, snapper and grouper throats (said to be the most tasty and tender part of the fish), and a local delicacy called fish roe. Available only in October and November, it is the eggs of fresh-water mullet.

Mullet, though not a rare item on Florida menus, is served quite differently here. Don't ask to see the owner (though many do) when you discover the entire skeleton, including tail, lying alongside your fillets. It is popular in this area to bread, fry and serve mullet backbones. Pieces of meat remain on the bones, particularly along the spine, after filleting. Locals love to munch on them, a whole plate at a time.

Soups include Seafood Gumbo and a thick Oyster Stew. There are ten sandwich choices including shrimp salad, crab and fried oyster.

The Stuffed Tomato has a flavorful stuffing of jalapeno cheese, sausage, green pepper, onion, crackers and croutons topped with chili powder. It's a refreshing change from the usual and can be substituted for the potato in your dinner order. Dinners come with salad, crackers with homemade garlic spread, hushpuppies or rolls, and your choice of fries, potato or grits.

Bell jars with seasoned croutons and bacon bits are kept

filled on the tables, as well as wine bottles containing Carolyn's popular homemade dressing.

Another departure from the norm is that you are permitted — actually encouraged — to bring your own liquor, beer or wine.

The proportions of food you receive leave little room for "Mom's" desserts. But if you can, "sit a spell," and order a piece of Rum Carrot Cake chock full of raisins and nuts; apple, pecan, coconut or Key Lime pie; or Chocolate-Peanut Butter Pie, a house specialty that allows the chunky peanut butter to remain in its natural state in a layer over the crust. You'll love it!

Carolyn compares her function in the kitchen to that of a wild scientist in a chemistry lab. She creates and concocts her recipes without regard for Fannie Farmer's do's and don'ts of culinary experimentation. The results are highly successful. Carolyn's husband, mother, mother-in-law, son, daughter and son-in-law free Carolyn of other restaurant duties to allow her to dedicate her 15-hour days to the cooking.

The Spring Creek Restaurant draws most of its clientele from Tallahassee, just a 45-minute scenic and unpopulated drive away. Guests have included legislators and government personnel who, though they could afford high-priced luxury, appreciate Carolyn's abundant home-cooked meals and her belief that it is better to get a slow nickel than a fast dime.

How to get there: Take Hwy. 363 south from Tallahassee. Head west on U.S. 98. Turn left on Hwy. 365, which will "drop you off" at the restaurant's doorstep.

While you're here: The beauty of Spring Creek's attractions list is that there aren't any. Enjoy doing nothing but appreciating the primitive surroundings and the anesthetic absence of noise pollution.

CHEESE STUFFED TOMATOES

3	large tomatoes (hearty type)
3	sausage patties (cooked, crumbled) or 5 slices bacon cooked and crumbled
	drippings from sausage or bacon
4	oz. Jalapeno cheese (grated)
½	c. green pepper (diced)
½	c. onion (diced)
¼	c. dry onion flakes
½	t. granulated garlic
½	t. seasoned salt
2	T. sugar
2	c. croutons (may substitute day-old bread cubes or cracker pieces)
	chili powder

1. Wash tomatoes. Cut in half and scoop out pulp. Place halves in baking dish.
2. Place pulp in large bowl. Add all of the above ingredients except chili powder. Mix well.
3. Stuff tomato halves, mounding the stuffing. Sprinkle with chili powder.
4. Bake in 350°F oven for 15 minutes.

Serves: 6
Preparation: 20 minutes
Cooking: 15 minutes

"It's easy to make a meal of these!"

— NOTES —

FRIED CORN

6 ears fresh corn (at room temperature)
3 lbs. "all-purpose" cooking fat
(or enough to cover corn)

1. Pull husks and silk from corn. Break ears in half.
2. Heat fat for deep fat frying to 350°F in a 3-4 quart kettle. Test for temperature with thermometer. If you don't have one, drop a 1-inch bread cube into hot fat. If cube browns in 60 seconds the fat will be about 350°F.
3. Very carefully drop corn into fat. Cook until ears are brown and crunchy on outside kernels.

Serves: 4-6
Preparation: 5 minutes
Cooking: 10 minutes

"A fun way to serve corn!"

— NOTES —

SPRING CREEK JALAPENO CHEESE GRITS

4	c. water
1	t. salt
1	c. grits
¼	c. margarine
4	oz. Jalapeno cheese (diced)
1	egg (beaten)
⅓	c. evaporated milk
2	dashes tabasco sauce
¼	c. bread crumbs
	paprika

1. In large saucepan, heat water and salt to boiling. Add grits.
2. Reduce heat and slowly cook until almost done. Stir several times.
3. Add margarine and cheese. Stir until melted.
4. Add egg, milk, and tabasco sauce. Stir until well mixed.
5. Grease a 1½-quart casserole. Add grits. Cover top with bread crumbs. Sprinkle with paprika.
6. Bake at 350 °F for 30 minutes.

Serves: 6
Preparation: 10 minutes
Cooking: 20-30 minutes

"Spicy and hot . . . you'll love it!"

— NOTES —

FRIED MULLET AND BACKBONE

4   **mullet fillets (from small to medium fish)**
     seasoned salt
1   **c. cracker meal**
     oil for frying
     backbone with tail attached from fillets

1. Sprinkle mullet fillets with seasoned salt.
2. Pat cracker meal on fillets to cover.
3. Heat oil to 350°F. Deep fat fry fillets for 10 minutes.
4. Take fishback and tail bones and dip in cracker meal. Fry for 5 minutes.
5. Serve fillets and backbones together.

Serves: 2-4
Preparation: 10 minutes
Cooking: 20 minutes

"This dish is unique to the area. They eat the meat off the bones along with the cracker meal. Try it before passing judgment!"

— NOTES —

249

CHOCOLATE PEANUT BUTTER PIE

1½ c. sugar
¼ c. cornstarch
1 t. flour
⅔ c. cocoa (or 3 squares unsweetened melted chocolate)
¼ t. salt
2¼ c. whole milk
¾ c. evaporated milk
4 egg yolks, beaten well
1 t. butter
1¼ t. vanilla
1 9" baked pie shell, cooled
1-1½ c. chunky style peanut butter
   whipped cream (topping)

1. In medium saucepan, mix sugar, cornstarch, flour, cocoa, salt. Stir until well mixed.
2. Blend the milks together. Pour a little at a time into the saucepan until consistency of a smooth paste. Add remaining milk, stirring well.
3. Add egg yolks and butter. Cook over low heat, stirring constantly until thickened.
4. Remove from heat, add vanilla, stir well. Set aside to cool.
5. Spread peanut butter over the bottom of cooled pie shell and up sides of shell.
6. Pour cooled chocolate mixture into pie shell and refrigerate.
7. Cut into serving portions and top with whipped cream.

Serves: 8
Preparation: 15 minutes/1 hour to chill
Cooking: 20 minutes
Chill: 2 hours

"A creamy, delicious and unusual dessert!"

— NOTES —

Wakulla Springs Lodge, Wakulla Springs, Florida

Wakulla Springs Lodge

— Wakulla Springs —

Wakulla Springs is 7,000 acres of what this country must have looked like before man rearranged things to his convenience. Virgin hardwood and pine forest, live oak, maples, cypress and magnolias rule the land. The only time a tree ever fell to the ground here was by nature's command.

Aside from the proprietor of the property, there to protect rather than intrude, only birds and wildlife are permitted to establish residency.

The red tile roof of the Spanish-style lodge in the heart of this paradise is the only evidence of mankind's existence. But its function is pure in nature as well, designed to house those who will appreciate the natural surroundings rather than exploit them. There is no bar in the Lodge, nor television in any of the 25 rooms.

Built in the 1930s, the Lodge is an architectural wonder. All floors, steps, desk tops, baseboards, offices and bathroom walls are marble. The 60-foot-long soda fountain in one wing is also made entirely of Tennessee marble. Woodwork is southern cypress. And the beams in the lobby are intricately decorated with Aztec and Toltec Indian designs, along with scenes of the river created by a local artist. Tables on the spacious porch are black granite, and priceless Spanish tiles adorn the area between the porch and lobby.

At the west end of the Lodge is the gracious, spacious dining room overlooking the Springs. It is very Southern in both atmosphere and offerings. Reminiscent of plantation days, the menu features fried chicken, blackeyed peas, grits, cornbread and the Lodge's famous Navy Bean Soup, described as a meal in itself. Entrees include Jumbo Shrimp wrapped in bacon and broiled with tomatoes, Stuffed Cornish Hens, Country Ham Steak, Mullet, Frog Legs, Crab Cakes and Apalachicola Oysters.

To maintain the "Old Guard" Southern formality of dining, no sandwiches are offered. Though prices are quite reasonable, the decor and service are elegant. Tablesettings show a special touch with cut crystal goblets and condiment containers, and complete silverware settings including three forks. French windows measuring 25 feet allow an unobstructed view of the natural surroundings.

Chef Gernard Gowdy has been preparing food since 1949 when he worked part-time in the Wakulla Springs Kitchen. He later accepted positions in Pennsylvania, Virginia, Ohio and several restaurants in Florida but recently returned to the Lodge, bringing with him nearly 25 years of experience.

Joseph R. Wilke, vice-president and general manager of Wakulla Springs, is the sole human being with permanent residence in this wildlife sanctuary. He is also designated as the Deputy Sheriff, Postmaster, Janitor and Game Warden for the 1,500 acres permitted to be hunted. Mr. Wilke was appointed to this position by the Edward Ball Wildlife Foundation following a career as an accountant for the St. Joe Paper Company, one of the late Mr. Ball's many business ventures. The Springs are a part of the financier's estate. Though the Lodge was his personal retreat, it has always been open to the public. Mr. Wilke's high regard for the self-made billionaire is the reason for his personal dedication to preserving the Lodge without change. He has also spent several years exploring the area's fascinating history, which is currently being reconstructed in a series of exhibits in a museum he has designed on the premises.

The beauty of Wakulla Springs, an Indian word meaning "mysteries of strange water," is said by many to be a Wonder of the World. Its crystal-clear waters are fed by an underground river whose basin covers four and a half acres with a maximum depth of 185 feet. The natural aquarium's clarity and the area's primitive beauty are among the reasons it was selected as the filming location for *The Creature of the Black Lagoon*, several Tarzan films and the underwater scenes for *Airport 77*.

How to get there: *Take U.S. 319 south from Tallahassee to Highway 61. Turn east on State Road 267 to entrance.*

While you're here: *The only man-made attractions at Wakulla Springs are the Jungle Cruise and the Glass-Bottom Boat Ride. Each, however, was designed to allow guests to experience nature's finest performance. You'll see many of the 154 species of birds recorded here as well as alligators, black bears, deer and wild turkeys, and Henry, the Pole-Vaulting Fish, a world-famous attraction.*

NAVY BEAN SOUP

1	lb. dried navy beans
5	c. water
1	can beef consomme
1	chicken bouillon cube
4	potatoes (diced)
2	onions (diced)
¼	c. butter
4	carrots
2	c. chopped ham
3	bay leaves
	salt and pepper to taste

1. Place navy beans, water, consomme, and bouillon cube in large pot. Bring to boil and then simmer for 2 hours.
2. Add potatoes to soup pot. Saute onions in butter until partially cooked. Add to soup pot along with everything else.
3. Simmer 1 hour or until vegetables are done. Serve.

Serves: 6
Preparation: 15 minutes
Cooking: 3 hours

"Serve with Cuban bread and green salad for a very nutritious meal!"

— NOTES —

CRAB IMPERIAL

---

1   lb. crab meat (best to use fresh — pick through to remove cartilage)
2   stalks celery (minced)
⅓   c. mayonnaise
1   t. lemon juice (fresh)
¼   t. salt
¼   t. Accent
2   dashes Worcestershire sauce
½   t. granulated garlic
     cracker crumbs
     Parmesan cheese

1. Butter casserole dish. Combine all ingredients above, except bread crumbs and cheese, in bowl. Mix well.
2. Let sit 1 hour. Place in buttered casserole dish. Top with cracker crumbs, Parmesan cheese. Dot with butter.
3. Bake in 350°F oven for 20 minutes.

Serves: 4
Preparation: 1 hour 15 minutes
Cooking: 20 minutes

"A light and delicate casserole!"

— NOTES —

STUFFED CORNISH HENS SUPREME
WITH WILD RICE

2	Cornish hens
½	bunch scallions (chopped)
½	c. fresh mushrooms (chopped)
1	c. prepared bread crumbs
⅓	c. sour cream
1	hard boiled egg (chopped)
	salt and pepper
	garlic butter

— SUPREME SAUCE —
drippings from hens

½	c. butter
¼	c. scallions (chopped)
½	c. fresh mushrooms (sliced)
½	c. flour
	milk
	salt and pepper
½	t. granulated garlic
½	t. nutmeg

— WILD RICE —

1	pkg. wild rice
	water
	butter

— BIRDS —

1. Clean and rinse birds. Mix scallions, mushrooms, bread crumbs, sour cream, and egg together in bowl.
2. Gently stuff birds making sure not to pack stuffing too tightly.
3. Salt and pepper birds. Apply garlic butter to outside of birds. Place breast side up in flat baking dish.
4. Cover dish with aluminum foil and bake in 350°F oven for 45 minutes.

5. At the end of cooking time, remove the foil drain drippings and put birds back to brown.

— SUPREME SAUCE —

6. Combine drippings and butter in small saute pan. Saute scallions and mushrooms until tender.
7. Add flour, stir until paste is formed. Add milk until desired sauce consistency.
8. Add seasonings.

— WILD RICE —

9. Cook rice according to package directions using proper amounts of water and butter.
10. Serve cornish hens on bed of wild rice with supreme sauce over top.

Serves: 2-4
Preparation: 20 minutes
Cooking: 1 hour

"A delightful dish that any cook would be proud to serve!"

— NOTES —

If you enjoyed *FAMOUS FLORIDA!*™ *Underground Gourmet* you'll love:

The secrets behind the specialty dishes of Florida's famous restaurants available in the exciting 320-page cookbook and guide entitled *FAMOUS FLORIDA!*™ *Restaurants & Recipes*. Enjoy, in your own home, delectable favorites such as: Louis Pappas' *Greek Salad* from his famous restaurant in Tarpon Springs, *Seafood-Mushroom Soup with Sherry* from Chalet Suzanne in Lake Wales, *Rack of Lamb Breakers from The* Breakers in Palm Beach, *Steak Tartare* from Bern's Steak House in Tampa, and the coveted recipe for *Hearts of Palm Salad with Sherbet Dressing* from the Captain's Table in Cedar Key.

ORDER FORM

Send to: LaFRAY PUBLISHING COMPANY,
P.O. Box 7326, St. Petersburg, Florida 33734
Phone: (813) 821-3233

Please send me:

_____ copies of *FAMOUS FLORIDA!*™
Restaurants & Recipes @ $9.95 each $ _____
_____ copies of *FAMOUS FLORIDA!*™
Underground Gourmet @ $9.95 each $ _____
Add postage and handling @ $1.50 each $ _____
Florida residents add 5% sales tax @ $.55 each $ _____
TOTAL ENCLOSED $ _____

- -

Send to: LaFRAY PUBLISHING COMPANY,
P.O. Box 7326, St. Petersburg, Florida 33734
Phone: (813) 821-3233

Please send me:

_____ copies of *FAMOUS FLORIDA!*™
Restaurants & Recipes @ $9.95 each $ _____
_____ copies of *FAMOUS FLORIDA!*™
Underground Gourmet @ $9.95 each $ _____
Add postage and handling @ $1.50 each $ _____
Florida residents add 5% sales tax @ $.55 each $ _____
TOTAL ENCLOSED $ _____

- -

Send to: LaFRAY PUBLISHING COMPANY,
P.O. Box 7326, St. Petersburg, Florida 33734
Phone: (813) 821-3233

Please send me:

_____ copies of *FAMOUS FLORIDA!*™
Restaurants & Recipes @ $9.95 each $ _____
_____ copies of *FAMOUS FLORIDA!*™
Underground Gourmet @ $9.95 each $ _____
Add postage and handling @ $1.50 each $ _____
Florida residents add 5% sales tax @ $.55 each $ _____
TOTAL ENCLOSED $ _____

PRINTS OF
FAMOUS FLORIDA!™

8" x 10"

The full-page scenes in this book are available signed by the artist and are excellent for framing.

One packet of 12 scenes is $15 including postage and handling. Make checks payable to:

Florida Prints
LaFray Publishing
P.O. Box 7326
St. Petersburg, FL 33734

GLOSSARY OF TERMS

Al dente — To cook until barely tender, such as pasta.

Blanch — To parboil and then shock in cold water.

Bechamel (see Cream Sauce)

Brown Sauce/Sauce Espanole — A rich beef stock reduced and thickened with roux. May be purchased as beef gravy.

Beurre Manie — 1 t. flour mixed with 1 t. butter — for thickening soups and sauces. Make a dozen of these little balls and freeze to be used as needed.

Butterfly — To cut against the grain or cut lengthwise, leaving meat attached on one side. This is done for appearance and to tenderize.

Caramelize — To melt sugar until it is liquid and light brown.

Chop/Dice/Mince —
Chop = ¼" cubes
Dice = ⅛" cubes
Mince = smallest cubes

Clarify/Clarified — To make butter clear by heating and removing all whey or sediment as it rises to the top. Then carefully strain.

Court Bouillon — Highly seasoned fish broth (see fish stock)

Cream Sauce/or Bechamel — White sauce made with milk.
1 T. butter
1 cup hot milk
1 T. flour
    salt, pepper, nutmeg to taste
1. Make roux of butter and flour. Cook until frothy, about 2 minutes.
2. Remove from heat. Slowly whisk in hot milk until smooth.
3. Cook 1 minute more and season.
    Yield: 1 cup

Cream Sauce is Bechamel made with cream instead of milk.
Veloute is Bechamel made with white stock (such as chicken, veal or fish) in place of milk.

Crepes — Thin pancakes (use blender or food processor)
- 3-4 eggs
- 1 cup flour
- 1½ cups milk
- ½ t. salt
- 3 T. butter (melted)

1. Combine all ingredients in processor and blend until smooth. Allow batter to rest 1 hour before frying. May be kept in refrigerator for 1 week.
2. 2 T. for each crepe in a 6-inch pan.

De-glaze — To pour liquid (such as wine, water or stock) in a cooking pan, scraping sides and bottom to loosen residue used in sauce.

Demi-Glaze — Half-glaze/A reduced brown sauce.

Dredge/Dust/Flour — To dip in or sprinkle lightly with flour.

Fillet/Filet — Boneless meat or fish. To remove bones from fish.

Fish Stock/Court Bouillon — Trimmings and scraps from fish
- 1-2 onions
- parsley stems, 1 carrot, 1 stalk celery
- 1 cup white wine
- 2 cups water

1. Simmer 20 minutes and strain.

Flambe/Flame — To cover food lightly with spirits and carefully ignite. It is to add flavor or spectacular beauty when serving.

Hollandaise Sauce (Blender)
- 3 egg yolks
- dash of cayenne
- 2 t. lemon juice
- ½ cup butter (melted)
- ¼ t. salt

1. In blender or food processor, beat yolks until thickened. Beat in juice, salt and cayenne.
2. Pour in hot butter, in a stream with machine running. Serve in a warmed bowl.

   Yield: 1 cup

Hollandaise Sauce (Classic)
¾ cup butter
4 t. lemon juice
3 egg yolks (beaten)
dash of salt & cayenne
1. In top of double boiler, melt ⅓ butter. Beat in eggs and juice with wire whisk.
2. Add remaining butter slowly, beating constantly until mixture thickens — never allowing water to boil.
3. Stir in seasonings and serve.

Yield: ¾ cup

Julienne — To cut into thin matchstick-like strips.

Poach — To simmer gently in hot liquid, to cover.

Puree — To force food through a sieve or blend in food processor until smooth.

Reduce — To cook or simmer a liquid until it is less; to concentrate flavor.

Roux — An equal amount of butter and flour cooked a few minutes until smooth. Used to thicken.

Saute — To cook in shallow pan, in small amount of butter or fat.

Score — To make shallow cuts in surface of meat.

Zest — Grated rind of citrus.

Index